Tomato

Tomato

GAIL HARLAND
SOFIA LARRINUA-CRAXTON

London, New York, Melbourne,
Munich, and Delhi

Editor Andrew Roff
Designer Kathryn Wilding
Senior Art Editor Susan Downing
Managing Editor Dawn Henderson
Managing Art Editor Christine Keilty
Senior Jacket Creative Nicola Powling
Production Editor Ben Marcus
Production Controller Wendy Penn
Creative Technical Support Sonia Charbonnier

US Editor Christy Lusiak
US Consultants Trevor Cole, Peggy Fallon

Photography
Sarah Ashun Graham Rae
William Reavell Howard Rice

DK India
Head of Publishing Aparna Sharma
Art Director Shefali Upadhyay
Designer Neha Ahuja
DTP Designer Tarun Sharma
Production Manager Pankaj Sharma

First American Edition, 2009
Published in the United States by
DK Publishing
375 Hudson House
New York, New York 10014

09 10 11 12 10 9 8 7 6 5 4 3 2 1

TD441—May 2009

A catalog record for this book is available from the Library
of Congress.

ISBN 978-0-7566-5094-0

DK books are available at special discounts when purchased in bulk for
sales promotions, premiums, fund-raising, or educational use. For
details, contact: DK Publishing Special Markets, 375 Hudson Street,
New York, New York 10014 or
SpecialSales@dk.com.

Color reproduction by MDP, UK

Printed and bound in China
by Hung Hung Printing

Discover more at
www.dk.com

Contents

The tomato story   6

The tomatoes   8

The plant 10 • The leaves 12 • The fruits 13 • The flavor 14
The benefits 15 • Best for sauces and salsas 16 • Best for soups 18
Best for salads 20 • Standard globe 22 • Cherry 36 • Beefsteak 52
Plum 64 • Weird and wonderful 74

In the garden   78

A tomato for every climate 80 • Where should I grow my tomatoes? 82
Preparing the soil 88 • Seed or plantlet? 90 • How to sow seeds 92
The first few weeks ... 94 • Toughening up 96 • Planting 98 • Crop rotation
102 • A little help from friends 104 • Mulching 106 • Food and drink 108
Removing sideshoots 110 • Pollination 112 • Pests and diseases 114
What's wrong with my leaves? 116 • What's wrong with my tomatoes? 118
Reaping the harvest 120 • Save your favorite seeds 124 • All for show 126
Get grafting 128 • Create a variety of your very own 130

In the kitchen   132

Preparation 134 • Cooking 140 • Preserving 142 • The recipes 144

Glossary and Useful resources 186
Index 188
Acknowledgments 192

The tomato story

Tangy, acidic, sweet, and juicy—the tomato's flavor profile puts it in prime position in kitchens around the world. But there is more to a tomato than its taste ...

Discovering the "golden apple"

Tomatoes originated in the coastal highlands of western South America where they were grown by the Aztecs and Mayans. They grow wild in Ecuador, northern Chile, Peru, and the Galapagos Islands—they are thought to have been brought here in the stomachs of turtles. The first written description of tomatoes, by the Italian Pietro Andrea Matthiola in 1544, referred to them as *Mala aurea*, or "golden apples." However, their close relationship to poisonous plants, such as the woody nightshade vine, meant they didn't receive the same regard when introduced more widely. (This suspicion isn't completely unfounded—tomato leaves do contain the poisonous chemical tomatine.) The tomato's great flavor didn't hide for long, however, and it soon became a welcome addition to cuisines around the world.

A wealth of varieties

New varieties arose by natural cross-pollination and selection, bringing us the largest beefsteaks to the smallest cherry tomatoes. Now, with over 5,000 varieties of all shapes and sizes, you will be able to find ones that suit your taste and planting space—whether its a sunny windowsill, pot, plot, or patio—perfectly. Healthy, easy to grow, and easy to care for, it's no wonder they are the most popular home crop. Use the following pages to choose which varieties to grow, then find out how best to nurture them, and finally choose a recipe that will allow you to enjoy your harvest in all its glory ...

Exotic Fruiting tomato plants are a beautiful sight in the garden—no wonder they are sometimes referred to as "love apples."

The
tomatoes

Choose from the following tomato varieties to decide what to grow, nurture, and enjoy. Think about where you will be growing your tomatoes, how much space you can give them, and in what types of recipes you wish to enjoy them. Please note, the tomatoes in the following pages are categorized according to their shape and size and categories may differ in other sources.

Key

◯   dwarf (low-growing bush)

▽   bush (determinate)

⌇   cordon (indeterminate)

☼   grows well in warm climates

☽   grows well in moderate climates

☀   grows well in cool climates

Heirloom – old/treasured open-pollinated plant
F1 hybrid – first generation plant resulting from crossing two pure-breeding parents
Hybrid – modern/commercial open-pollinated plant
No. of days – days from planting until fruits mature

The plant

The tomato plant is a short-lived annual that thrives in temperate regions. Plants grow very differently, so don't worry about not having enough space—there is a plant for every sized pot (or plot!)

Tomato plants range in height from tiny plants just 6in (15cm) tall to vines that can reach 30ft (10m), although 8ft (2.5m) is usual. There are three main growth habits: dwarf, bush, and cordon.

Dwarf types, such as 'Tiny Tim' (p37) and 'Micro-Tom' (p43), have a dwarfing gene, which makes these compact plants ideal for growing in containers. Many dwarf plants look very ornamental when in full bloom.

Bush types, such as 'Siberian' (p34) and 'Roma' (p65), are called determinates, as they usually grow to a fixed height. A bush has no prominent leading shoot. Instead, it has a number of sideshoots, each ending in a fruit truss, which form a bushy, often sprawling plant. It usually fruits in one flush and so is useful for commercial because it is easy to harvest altogether.

Cordon, or vine plants, such as 'Jubilee' (p22) and 'Extra Sweetie' (p46), are indeterminates, as their growth height is not fixed. These vigorous plants have one stem that continues to flower and fruit, on trusses from the main stem, over a long season until it is killed by frost.

A few plants have variable habits and are called semi-bush, or semi-determinate, types. They usually reach a set height like bush tomatoes, but produce a second crop.

Heirlooms, F1 hybrids, and hybrids

Tomato plants are often classed as either heirloom or hybrid varieties. There are many definitions of these terms, with some people maintaining that heirloom plants must have been grown for at least 50 years (or even 100 years). Others argue that true heirlooms are those that have been passed down through generations of a single family. Many so-called heirlooms are recent creations but have attracted the title, as they are unlikely to be commercially successful, and so their survival depends on gardeners saving their seeds. In this book, the term heirloom is used in its widest sense to refer to any open-pollinated variety that is particularly treasured or has a known heritage.

F1 hybrid plants are the first generation that result from crossing two selected pure-breeding parents. They are commercially produced and seeds saved from these plants will not breed true, so the seedlings may vary and be of a lower quality.

There are also a number of modern or commercial open-pollinated varieties here called hybrids. They were originally produced by cross-breeding genetically distinct parents but have been stabilized so that open-pollinated seeds will usually produce offspring like the parent plant.

GROWTH HABITS – choose a type to suit the way you wish to grow it

Dwarf Most dwarf plants grow to a very small size and are ideal for growing on a patio or windowsill.

Bush These short and shapely plants have many sideshoots, which means the plant sprawls out in all directions.

Cordon These long and upright plants produce a range of fruit shapes and colors. Their fruiting season is longer too.

The leaves

Most gardeners do not consider the foliage of the tomato plant, but the leaves of some are quite distinctive and can cause the plant to have an increased resistance to disease.

The regular tomato leaf is composed of a number of leaflets, each of which has a serrated, irregular edge, or margin.

Potato-leafed plants, such as 'Hillbilly Potato Leaf' (p53), may have a few lobes on their leaves, but generally the edges are smooth. They are slightly thicker than those of regular tomato plants, and they therefore may be more resistant to some diseases.

Some plants, such as 'Green Sausage' (p77), have more finely divided leaves than others; the Russian heirloom 'Silvery Fir Tree' (p28) is particularly known for its very fine leaves. The plant 'Variegated,' thought to have originated in Ireland, has leaves irregularly splashed with cream. Most attractive for their foliage are plants such as 'Elberta Girl' and 'Velvet Red' (p43); these have leaves so densely covered in silvery hairs that they are quite furry to the touch. This type of leaf is sometimes called an angora leaf, after the tomato variety of that name. It is important to keep an eye on the foliage of your tomato plants as they grow, because the first signs of many problems can occur there (pp114–117).

LEAF TYPES – don't reach straight for the fruit, the leaves like to show off too!

Regular Most plants, such as 'Ildi,' have leaves with a toothed margin.

Potato A leaf form with smooth edges that may be more resistant to disease.

Serrated Some plants have quite fine leaves, such as 'Green Sausage.'

Angora Covered in fine silvery hairs, these plants repel insect attack.

The fruits

Tomato fruits vary in size from currant tomatoes that weigh less than ¼oz (5g) to monster beefsteaks of 2lb (1kg) or more. They can also be found in a rainbow of colors from creamy white to deep purple.

Shapes and sizes

Tomatoes are usually classified according to their shape and size. The familiar round tomato is the standard globe. Small round tomatoes are known as cherries, and those slightly bigger, such as 'Garcia,' usually marketed on the vine, are called cocktail tomatoes. Very tiny fruits are referred to as currant tomatoes. Beefsteak tomatoes can sometimes be the size of a small pumpkin and have a flattened globelike appearance with beautifully ribbed bodies. Plum tomatoes are used traditionally in Italy for preserving and have an elongated, plum shape. Mini-plum tomatoes of the 'Santa' type have become very popular in recent years for snacking.

(In this book, mini-plums can be found in the Plum section, although other sources may classify them as cherries.) There are other shapes of tomato that do not fit easily into a category; in this book, you'll find these in the Weird and wonderful section.

Color

Although most people think of tomatoes as red, they can also be yellow, orange, green, white, nearly black or brown, and various shades of maroon-purple. The fruits may be a single color, speckled or striped with a different color, or multicolored, like 'Big Rainbow' (p63).

SEED CHAMBERS – also known as locules, these are usually constant in varieties

Bilocular fruits Most cherry tomatoes, such as 'Nectar' (p42), contain just two seed chambers.

Trilocular fruits Three seed chambers are common in standard varieties, such as 'Alaskan Fancy' (p66).

Multilocular fruits These are particularly common in beefsteak varieties, such as 'Ananas Noir' (p55).

The flavor

For many people, growing their own tomatoes is all about the flavor. Store-bought tomatoes often taste disappointing compared to home-grown crops, but the reasons behind this are complex.

Perceived flavor is derived from a combination of taste and smell. Over 400 volatile compounds have been identified in tomatoes, of which about 30 are thought to contribute to aroma.

The traditional sweet-sour taste of a tomato results from the sugar and organic-acid content of the fruit. Some tomatoes have a higher sugar content than others; for example, 'Black Cherry' contains twice as much sugar as the oxheart 'Sterling Old Norway.' Sugar content, however, can vary with season and the ripeness of the fruit. The flavor of tomatoes ripening in the increased sunlight of high summer is usually better than that of earlier crops.

For many years, commercial tomatoes have often been harvested when green and

Green Zebra (p26)

then exposed to ethylene gas to ripen them in storage. Tomatoes ripened on the vine are thought to have a much better flavor, although much of the aroma is released by the vine itself. Fruits nibbled while you work among the plants often taste best of all.

The tastiest of them all?

There is no doubt that flavor varies greatly between tomatoes. White and yellow fruits are generally less acidic than red tomatoes. Many black- and brown-fruited plants are praised for their more complex flavors.

Varieties that are regularly commended as particularly flavorsome include the mini-plum 'Floridity' (p70), yellow cherry 'Snowberry' (p40), beefsteak 'Brandywine' (p59) in its various incarnations, the French 'Carmello,' 'Green Zebra,' and 'Black Prince.'

Black Cherry (p38)

The benefits

Tomatoes can play an important role in the diet. They are a valuable source of vitamins A and C, as well as several minerals, including calcium, iron, manganese, and, particularly, potassium.

Tomatoes contain an average of 0.09mg of vitamin A and 15mg of vitamin C per 4oz (100g) of fruit, as well as 397mg of potassium per 100mg of fruit. They also contain lycopene, which is a carotenoid (a pigment involved in photosynthesis) that gives red coloring to tomatoes, pink

Favorita
(p37)

grapefruit, and watermelons. Several population studies have indicated that diets high in lycopene may offer protection against certain cancers.

Lycopene in tomatoes can be absorbed more effectively by the body when the tomatoes have been processed in some way, particularly when they are combined with fat and heated—so drizzling olive oil over your tomatoes and roasting them should be especially beneficial.

A balanced diet

Lycopene is found in higher concentrations in red tomatoes; in studies, one cherry tomato of the variety 'Favorita' contained 1.39mg of lycopene, compared with 0.14mg found in a 'Golden Cherry' (p39) fruit. However, orange tomatoes have their own benefits—they have been found to contain much more vitamin A, in the form of beta-carotene, than red tomatoes.

There is no doubt that selecting and eating a variety of different tomatoes, of different shapes, sizes, and colors, as part of your diet will give you the best possible balance of nutrients. What more excuse do you need?

Aviro
(p66)

Best for sauces and salsas

Sauces and salsas are only as good as the tomatoes that go into them, so if you're planning to use your harvest to make up pots and pots of saucy delights, choose which tomato varieties you want to grow wisely. Here are some of the best of the bunch.

Sauces

Ripe plum tomatoes are the best for sauces because they have a good balance of flesh and juice. They also have a savory quality that makes them very good for making flavorsome sauces. The plum 'San Marzano Lungo' is the traditional tomato of choice in Italian kitchens for superb sauces.

San Marzano Lungo (p65)

Floridity (p70)

Long Tom (p67)

Juliet (p69)

Cornue des Andes (p72)

Salsas

For salsas, the choice of tomato depends on the salsa in question. If you are making fresh salsa, use a plump, meaty variety—beefsteaks are good. If you are making a chargrilled or cooked salsa, you can use other kinds of tomatoes, such as plums and standard globes.

Big Boy (p58)

Maskotka (p46)

Stupice (p27)

Druzba (p32)

Eva's Purple Ball (p31)

Mule Team (p25)

Best for soups

Because tomatoes for soups are likely to be puréed, you need to look for ripeness and depth of flavor—ideal requests when you are dealing with a glut. Most plum tomatoes are an ideal foundation for a hearty tomato soup, particularly the varieties shown here. Add some cherry tomatoes to the mix for extra sweetness and playfulness.

San Marzano Lungo (p65)

Ruby (p48)

Cornue des Andes (p72)

Rudolph (p70)

Principe Borghese (p66)

Rosada (p70)

Long Tom (p67)

Floridity (p/U)

Tomatoberry (p46)

Loveheart (p41)

Nectar (p42)

Best for salads

For salads, both large plump beefsteaks and pretty little cherry tomatoes are ideal. Beefsteaks are fleshy, and they soak up the flavor of a good vinaigrette. They also combine well with other ingredients, giving texture to a salad. Cherries of different colors look pretty in salads, add sweetness, and hold their shape.

Costoluto Fiorentino (p57)

Supermarmande (p59)

Yellow Pigmy (p48)

Blue Ridge Mountain (p58)

Loveheart (p41)

Brandywine (p59)

Reisetomate (p77)

Riesentraube (p49)

German Pink (p61)

Golden Gem (p36)

Standard globe

When people think of tomatoes, it is usually the classic round tomatoes that come to mind. These generally vary between 3 and 4oz (70 and 100g) and have two to four seed cavities inside. They are more or less globe shaped with a regular outline and come in a rainbow of colors. The skin thickness, flesh texture, and flavor can also vary dramatically between varieties. Even fruits from a single plant can vary, so don't be surprised to find unusual tomatoes among your crop.

Jubilee

🌱 ☀️ **Heirloom, 72 days** Compact plants produce a good crop of orange tomatoes similar to the variety 'Sunray.' 'Jubilee' was an All-America Selections winner in 1943.

Characteristics Attractive, golden-yellow fruits with a somewhat dry flesh and low acidity. May grow to the size of a small beefsteak.

How to enjoy Often used for bottling and to make orange and tomato marmalade.

Roncardo

🌱 ☀️ **F1 hybrid, 75 days** This plant from Holland produces large tomatoes in clusters of 4–6. Shows good disease resistance.

Large fruits not always as regular as this

Characteristics Large, red, sweet fruits usually in the range of 4–5oz (100–150g), but some fruits may be larger beefsteak types.

How to enjoy Well-flavored fruits are perfect sliced in sandwiches or burgers.

Ferline

☀ ☀ ☀ **F1 hybrid, 75 days** Consistently heavy-cropping plant from France with excellent disease resistance, even outdoors.

Characteristics Solid, deep red tomatoes. They keep their texture well after picking. Sometimes classed as a beefsteak.

How to enjoy Good in sandwiches, because they remain firm after slicing.

Glacier

▽ ☀ ☀ **Heirloom, 65 days** Early potato-leafed plant introduced in Sweden in 1985. It is one of the most cold tolerant of all tomato plants. Produces a heavy crop.

Characteristics Flavorful, red globe tomatoes weighing just 2oz (50g) each. They have thick skins and very few seeds.

How to enjoy Better flavor than most early tomatoes, improves further grilled or roasted.

Few seeds

Shirley

☀ **F1 hybrid, 65 days** Very popular in England since the 1970s, 'Shirley' was first released in Israel. It is a reliable, early maturing plant, which produces more than 13lb (6kg) fruits. Ideal for unheated greenhouses or polytunnels.

Characteristics Very uniform, medium-sized fruits with a good texture and acidic taste.

How to enjoy Great for general kitchen use.

Very even-shaped fruits

Sungella

🌱 ☀️ **Heirloom, 70 days** Raised in Norfolk, England by a customer of Thompson and Morgan, who crossed the popular 'Sungold' (p41) with a larger fruited orange heirloom.

Characteristics Prolific crops of orange, golf ball-sized tomatoes, which are sweet and juicy.

How to enjoy Useful size to eat fresh but also good roasted with peppers and eggplant.

Bright orange, juicy fruits

Moneymaker

🌱 ☀️ ☀️ ☀️ **Heirloom, 70 days** Reliable English outdoor tomato raised by F. Stoner in Southampton, UK, also known for 'Stoner's Exhibition.' Strong plants are easy to grow in pots or the open ground.

Characteristics Good-looking, smooth, medium-sized, scarlet fruits.

How to enjoy Good for sauces and salsas.

Alicante

🌱 ☀️ ☀️ **Heirloom, 68 days** English bred, reliable, early cropper that was introduced by Suttons Seeds in 1966 for growing outdoors or under cover. Easy to grow even in dull summers.

Characteristics These attractive, red tomatoes are resistant to greenback (pp118–119).

How to enjoy The firm-textured fruits are excellent baked or roasted.

Sioux

☀ ☀ ☀ **Heirloom, 60 days** Compact
plants bred for use in the American plains
by the Department of Horticulture,
University of Nebraska in 1944, 'Sioux' also
does well in Northern Britain and Europe.

Characteristics Small- to medium-sized, deep
red tomatoes with a good flavor.

How to enjoy Try these well-flavored
tomatoes in salads early in the summer.

Tigerella

☀ ☀ **Heirloom, 60 days** Bred by
Dr. L. A. Derby in England around 1970.
This early maturing variety is sometimes
called 'Mr. Stripey,' which is actually the
name of an American striped beefsteak.

Characteristics Red-and-yellow-striped fruits
with a tangy taste.

How to enjoy Attractive, tangy tomatoes for
salads and sandwiches.

*Red skins with light
orange-yellow stripes*

Mule Team

☀ **Heirloom, 80 days** A reliable, old
plant from the US that is high yielding
and tolerant of many diseases.

Characteristics The bright red globes often
show a slight ribbing around the stalk. They
have a sweet and tangy taste.

How to enjoy Ideal for grilling or frying, and
making delicious salsas.

*Bright
red fruits*

Green Zebra

☀ ☼ ☼ **Hybrid, 75 days** Introduced in 1983 by Thomas P. Wagner of Tater Mater Seeds in the US.

Characteristics Yellowish green with deep green stripes, these attractive tomatoes have a tangy flavor and are resistant to splitting.

How to enjoy Serve cut into wedges as an interesting contrast to red tomatoes.

Fruits may vary in shape, usually less ribbed

Black Zebra

☀ ☼ **Hybrid, 85 days** A child of Tom Wagner's 'Green Zebra' (above), stabilized by Jeff Dawson in California and first introduced in 2000.

Characteristics An attractive novelty tomato with deep red-and-green-striped fruits, which, sadly, are not as tasty as they look.

How to enjoy Aside from its decorative qualities, try 'Black Zebra' in soups and sauces.

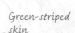

Green-striped skin

Deep red flesh

Orange Pixie

○ ☼ **Hybrid, 52 days** An attractive bushy plant growing to around 20in (50cm) in height only. It is an orange-fruited version of the red 'Pixie.'

Characteristics These distinctive orange fruits are slightly elongated globes with firm flesh and an excellent flavor.

How to enjoy Halve fruits and bake in the oven with a drizzle of olive oil.

Juicy fruits

The Amateur

▽ ☼ ☼ **Heirloom, 60 days** One of the best known British tomatoes, whose early cropping and good disease resistance makes it an excellent choice for beginners. Produces fruits reliably over a long season.

Characteristics Medium-sized, red tomatoes.

How to enjoy Useful everyday tomato for salads or frying.

Tamina

🌱 ☼ **Hybrid, 60 days** A potato-leafed plant raised by the German company Saatzucht Quedlingburg. Plants produce very few sideshoots.

Characteristics These very even globe fruits are a bright red color and have a good flavor.

How to enjoy Roast with plenty of olive oil, then sprinkle with feta cheese.

Stupice

🌱 ☼ ☼ **Heirloom, 65 days** Potato-leafed plant that is very popular in its native Czech Republic. Seed was sent to the US in 1977 by Milan Sodomka. Compact plants cope well in cold conditions.

Irregular-shaped fruits are fairly common

Characteristics Usually round tomatoes with a rich flavor.

How to enjoy Well-flavored tomatoes, excellent in soups, salsas, or stews.

Essex Wonder

☀ ☼ ☀ Heirloom, **75 days** Vigorous, potato-leafed English plant released by Dobie and Company for unheated greenhouse or outdoors. Ideal for planting in pots and growing bags, but can be rampant when planted in the ground.

Characteristics Firm-textured, scarlet fruits with a good flavor.

How to enjoy Ideal for grilling and frying.

Scotland Yellow

☀ ☼ ☀ Heirloom, **70 days** Vigorous plants that were bred in Scotland for growing in cooler climates. Very similar to 'Yellow Ailsa Craig'.

Characteristics These round, golden-yellow, juicy tomatoes have a sweet and tangy taste, and stay in good condition long after picking.

How to enjoy These tasty tomatoes make excellent sauces.

Bright yellow-colored fruits

Silvery Fir Tree

☀ ☼ Heirloom, **58 days** A traditional Russian plant with distinctive, finely dissected foliage, making an ornamental patio plant.

Characteristics Very juicy, round, red tomatoes with a rather tart flavor and lots of seeds.

How to enjoy Serve grilled or fried as a breakfast tomato.

Celebrity

☰ ☼ ☀ **Hybrid, 70 days** Vigorous, high-yielding bushy plants showing good disease resistance. This variety was an All-America Selections winner in 1984.

Characteristics Large, red tomatoes of reasonable flavor.

How to enjoy Roast with eggplant, peppers, and onions.

Pink Ping Pong

🌱 ☀ **Heirloom, 75 days** 'Ping Pong' is a Canadian variety bred in 1978 by the University of Manitoba in Winnipeg from 'Summit' and 'Red Cherry' (p40). The pink-fruiting strain is very prolific.

Characteristics The variety is so-named because the pink fruits are about the size of a ping-pong ball. Very sweet and juicy.

How to enjoy Ideal for snacking and salads.

Pink tinge to skin

Grosse Lisse

🌱 ☼ ☀ ☀ **Heirloom, 80 days** One of the most popular varieties in Australia, 'Grosse Lisse' is thought to have originated in Germany around 1870. The plant copes well with varying temperatures.

Characteristics The large, round fruits have thin skins and a meaty flesh with a pleasant, acidic taste.

How to enjoy Excellent in sandwiches.

Carters Fruit

※ ☀ **Heirloom, 75 days** Introduced by the seed company Carters of London, England, in the 1930s. This is a strong growing plant for indoors or outside.

Characteristics The skin of these crimson tomatoes has a distinctive powdery bloom.

How to enjoy These sweet, luscious fruits can be eaten as a dessert fruit.

Elegance

※ ☀ **F1 Hybrid, 72 days** Widely grown commercially as on-the-vine tomatoes, this plant from the Dutch firm De Ruiter Seeds is sometimes offered to amateur growers as grafted transplants to increase vigor.

Characteristics Perfectly shaped red tomatoes that are usually favored in taste trials.

How to enjoy Eat fresh in salads or use for richly colored gazpacho.

Perfectly round even fruits

First In The Field

▽ ☀ ☀ **Heirloom, 60 days** A very productive tomato released in the early twentieth century that crops early, and so often escapes attacks of blight. Plants are particularly tolerant to cold.

Characteristics Traditional red globe tomatoes with a firm texture and good flavor.

How to enjoy Savor these well-flavored tomatoes fresh early in the tomato season.

White Tomesol

🍴 ☀️ **Heirloom, 82 days** Of German origin, this is of a more regular shape than the similar 'White Queen.'

Characteristics Large, smooth-skinned, creamy white fruits weighing around 7oz (200g).

How to enjoy Some people find white tomatoes unappealing, but this variety has a pleasant citruslike taste and can be eaten like an apple.

Fairly dry flesh

Golden Sunrise

🍴 ☀️ **Heirloom, 72 days** Introduced by the English seed company Carters in the early 1890s, 'Golden Sunrise' is a popular classic tomato.

Characteristics The smooth, golden-yellow tomatoes have a low acidity, thin skins, and firm flesh.

How to enjoy A sweet-tasting, multipurpose salad tomato.

Eva's Purple Ball

🍴 ☀️ ☀️ **Heirloom, 70 days** An old German heirloom that was taken to New Jersey in the late nineteenth century by the family of Joseph J. Bratka. High-yielding plants show some tolerance of blight.

Characteristics Extremely sweet and juicy fruits are pinkish red (not purple) and evenly round when ripe.

How to enjoy Grill sliced or make a tasty salsa.

Druzba

🌱 ☀️ **Heirloom, 80 days** The word *druzhba* means friendship in Bulgarian. These disease-resistant plants reliably produce a prolific crop.

Characteristics These deep red globes have a well-balanced flavor.

How to enjoy Juicy fruits ideal for making into rich savory sauces and salsas.

Earl of Edgecombe

🌱 ☀️ ☀️ **Heirloom, 73 days** The seventh Earl of Edgcumbe was a New Zealand sheep farmer before claiming his title in 1965. He took this tomato to England with him.

Characteristics Uniform, deep orange globe tomatoes with a good flavor and not too many seeds.

How to enjoy Delicious raw but the firm, meaty flesh is also good for grilling and frying.

Rich orange-colored skin and flesh

Ailsa Craig

🌱 ☀️ **Heirloom, 80 days** First introduced in 1912 by Alexander and Brown of The Scottish Seed House, 'Ailsa Craig' was raised by Alan Balch as a cross between 'Fillbasket' and 'Sunrise.' Named after an isle in the Firth of Clyde.

Characteristics Blood red, smooth tomatoes, which are firm and juicy but fairly acidic.

How to enjoy Versatile; good for any dish.

Totem

○ ☼ **Hybrid, 75 days** Bred by the British company Floranova in 1996, this is a neat, very productive stocky bush ideal for pots or window boxes.

Characteristics Bright red tomatoes that can be rather small for standard globes. Sometimes classed as a cherry tomato.

How to enjoy Grow on a windowsill to have a ready supply of delicious snacking tomatoes.

Czech's Excellent Yellow

⌇ ☼ **Heirloom, 72 days** Introduced by Ben Quisenberry of Ohio in 1976, seeds of this variety probably came from Milan Sodomka of the Czech Republic, who sent seeds of other varieties including 'Czech's Bush.'

Characteristics These very smooth, round fruits are an attractive rich yellow color.

How to enjoy The soft-textured tomatoes are great when used in chutneys and pickles.

Long Keeper

▽ ☼ **Heirloom, 78 days** A semi-bush variety released by Burpee Seeds in the US. The tomatoes ripen slowly for 1–3 months after harvest.

Characteristics Orange-red tomatoes will store for 12 weeks or more in a cool, dry place.

How to enjoy Not the best flavored tomato, but convenient for winter use. Best cooked in soups and casseroles.

Distinctive orange-red skin

Cristal

☝ ☀ **F1 hybrid, 85 days** High-yielding plants that are very resistant to disease.

Characteristics Glossy, bright red tomatoes up to 4½oz (120g) in weight with a richly colored flesh and good flavor.

How to enjoy Excellent variety for eating in fresh salads and sandwiches.

Siberian

▽ ☀ ☀ **Heirloom, 48 days** Russian heirloom plant that sets fruit even at low temperatures and is productive even in short seasons.

Characteristics Bright red globe tomatoes.

How to enjoy Use in soups and stews or the first summer salads.

Rich red, succulent fruit

Sub-Arctic Plenty

○ ☀ ☀ **Heirloom, 50 days** Bred at the Beaverlodge Research Station in Alberta, Canada, in the 1970s, specifically for short season gardening in cool conditions. Sister varieties include 'Sub-Arctic Delight,' 'Sub-Arctic Maxi,' and 'Sub-Arctic Midi.'

Characteristics Bright scarlet fruits with a sweet and tangy taste.

How to enjoy Lovely roasted with thyme.

Lemon Boy

✿ ☼ **F1 hybrid, 72 days** Introduced by Petoseed in the US in 1984, the disease-resistant plants are generally very prolific.

Characteristics Large, bright lemon-yellow tomatoes with a low-acid flavor and not too many seeds.

How to enjoy Try using for colorful salsas and gazpacho.

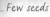

— Few seeds

Harzfeuer

✿ ☼ **F1 hybrid, 65 days** This early cropping plant from Germany is very popular with market gardeners. The name translates as "resin fire". Open-pollinated seed is sometimes listed.

Characteristics Large, round, red fruits have a slightly acidic flavor.

How to enjoy Good general purpose tomato for salads or cooking.

Flamme

✿ ☼ **Heirloom, 68 days** Also known as 'Jaune Flamme,' this is a prolific-cropping old and much-loved French plant.

Characteristics Beautiful, smooth, round fruits of a rich tangerine orange.

How to enjoy Wonderful grilled or roasted but also very good for drying.

Cherry

Small, roundish tomatoes are referred to as cherry tomatoes because their shape and size resemble the fruit of that name. They generally weigh around ½–1oz (10–20g), are usually roughly spherical with just two seed chambers, and have a high sugar content. Most varieties are easy to grow and trouble-free. The tiny fruits related to the wild species *Solanum pimpinellifolium* are called currant tomatoes. They weigh around 1/16oz (2g) and have a particularly sweet taste.

Tumbler

☰ ☀ **Hybrid, 55 days** German-bred trailing plant, which crops over a long period. One of the best tomato plants for cascading out of a hanging basket or a window box.

Characteristics Bright red cherry tomatoes with a sweet taste.

How to enjoy Ideal cooked on skewers for dishes such as shish kebabs.

Golden Gem

❦ ☀ **F1 hybrid, 65 days** A prolific tomato bred in China, which may have 20 to 70 fruits in a cluster.

Characteristics The golden-yellow fruits have a good flavor and a high sugar content of around 10 percent. They show some resistance to splitting.

Golden-yellow fruits

How to enjoy An ornamental cherry tomato—try using it to decorate a fruit salad.

Tiny Tim

○ ☀ **Hybrid, 50 days** Fast-maturing plants introduced in 1944, ideal for growing in window boxes or pots. Plants will fruit successfully in 6in (15cm) pots.

Characteristics The small, sweet tomatoes are reliably produced very early in the season.

How to enjoy Perfect patio plants, you can enjoy the fruits while relaxing in the sun.

Gartenperle

❦ ☀ **Heirloom, 68 days** 'Gartenperle,' translated as "garden pearl," is of German origin. It forms a dwarf-trailing bush ideal for growing in hanging baskets or patio pots and produces fruits in great profusion.

Characteristics These are small, sweet, pinkish red fruits.

How to enjoy Very popular variety with addictive fruits to nibble off the plant.

pinkish fruits

Favorita

❦ ☀ **F1 hybrid, 65 days** Vigorous disease-resistant plants, which will usually produce a good crop even in wet summers.

Characteristics Rich red cherry tomatoes held on long trusses. They have tough skins and a fairly acidic taste, which becomes sweeter in hot summers.

How to enjoy Cook in flans and quiches.

Fox Cherry

🌱 ☀️ **Heirloom, 80 days** This popular tomato is produced in large quantities over a long season on tall, disease-resistant plants.

Characteristics Large, red cherries weigh around 1¼oz (30g) each and have a rich, slightly acidic flavor.

How to enjoy Try serving these on skewers with mini-mozzarella balls and an aïoli dressing.

Relatively large cherries

Tommy Toe

🌱 ☼ ☼ ☼ **Heirloom, 70 days** From the Ozark Mountains in Arkansas. Widely distributed in Australia by Diggers Seeds, these long-cropping plants show good blight resistance.

Characteristics Voted top in taste trials, the large cherries have an excellent flavor.

How to enjoy Eat freshly picked from the vine or in salads.

Black Cherry

🌱 ☼ ☀️ **Heirloom, 65 days** Vigorous, high-yielding plants developed by Vince Sapp in the US. Released in 2003.

Characteristics Produces large clusters of dusky purplish, round tomatoes with a rich flavor and high sugar content. Can be prone to splitting.

How to enjoy Eat straight off the vine or mix with other cherry varieties for a colorful salad.

Chocolate Cherry

🌱 ☀️ **Heirloom, 70 days** Raised in the US, these plants produce masses of fruits, usually in clusters of eight.

Characteristics Looks similar to 'Black Cherry' (opposite) but is marginally larger and more resistant to splitting. Good flavor and a deep maroon-black color.

How to enjoy Lower in calories than real chocolate, this is the ideal sweet snack.

Thick skins

Golden Cherry

🌱 ☀️ **F1 hybrid, 60 days** Introduced by Suntech Seeds of Taiwan, this is a vigorous plant for greenhouses or outdoors. Produces long trusses of well-spaced fruits.

Characteristics These firm cherries are bright orange-yellow and have a very sweet, tangy taste.

How to enjoy The fruit's excellent flavor makes it particularly appealing to children.

Matt's Wild Cherry

🌱 ☀️ **Heirloom, 70 days** An early cropping currant of Mexican origin that was named after Matt Liebman. It is a vigorous sprawling plant, which will self-seed in the garden.

Characteristics The tiny, flavorful tomatoes weigh less than 1/16oz (3g) each. They have a firm texture and contain many seeds.

How to enjoy These exceedingly sweet and juicy fruits are best scattered over salads.

Plenty of seeds

Red Cherry

☀ **Heirloom, 65 days** An RHS report in 1877 noted that this tomato was a profusely fruiting, ornamental variety.

Characteristics Pinkish red, round fruits with a good sweet flavor. Some suppliers use this name for a mini-plum variety.

How to enjoy Popular as a snack or oven roasted with peppers and eggplant.

Glossy red skins

Snowberry

☀ **F1 hybrid, 75 days** Raised in The Netherlands by Sahin Seeds, this plant produces a heavy yield of fruits.

Characteristics The relatively large, attractive fruits are creamy yellow when mature and have a rich, sweet flavor with citrus hints.

How to enjoy Ideal for nibbling on as a snack between meals.

Creamy-yellow fruits

Jelly Bean

☀ **Hybrid, 66 days** Introduced in the US in 2007, there are red and yellow versions of this variety.

Characteristics Sweet, grapelike glossy fruits weighing about 1oz (20g) with 15–30 in a cluster. Good resistance to splitting and very long keeping.

How to enjoy Straight off the plant for a garden snack or will dry well for winter use.

Bright glossy fruits

Loveheart

¶ ☼ **F1 hybrid, 75 days** Also sold as CUTIE, this variety from Taiwan was first released in 2005. The fruits increasingly take on a heart shape as the plant matures.

Characteristics The rich red, heart-shaped fruits make this a very appealing choice, especially since they have a good tangy flavor.

How to enjoy Serve at a special dinner for the one you love!

Distinctly heart-shaped fruits

Sunset

¶ ☼ **F1 hybrid, 65 days** Productive hybrid that has been successful in recent trials. Healthy vines produce a good yield.

Characteristics Bright orange fruits are sweet and richly flavored.

How to enjoy The very ornamental fruits look particularly dramatic in a salad with 'Black Cherry' (p38) or 'Brown Berry' (p45).

Sungold

¶ ☼ ☼ **F1 hybrid, 60 days** Bred in Japan by the Tokita Seed Company, 'Sungold' was released in Britain and America in 1992 and rapidly became the most popular cherry tomato. The plants are very productive and have good virus resistance.

Characteristics Very sweet, golden-yellow, thin-skinned tomatoes.

How to enjoy Irresistible straight off the vine.

Thin skins

Sakura

☀ ☀ **F1 hybrid, 70 days** A modern high-yielding and early fruiting plant raised in The Netherlands. Plants produce long trusses of approximately 20 tomatoes.

Characteristics These uniform bright red cherries have a very sweet flavor.

How to enjoy Firm tasty fruits hold well on skewers to make savory kebabs or to dip in cheese fondue.

Bright red fruits

Nectar

☀ ☀ **F1 hybrid, 68 days** Modern early fruiting hybrid, from the seed company Enza Zaden in Holland, that grows best under glass.

Characteristics Tasty, glossy fruits on long trusses store well after harvest.

How to enjoy Good for roasting—bake in the oven with sausages, herbs, and garlic. Alternatively, add to a soup.

Glossy skins

Gardener's Delight

☀ ☀ ☀ **Heirloom, 75 days** One of the best known of all tomatoes, 'Gardener's Delight,' or 'Sugar Lump,' is of German origin, bred by Paul Tellhelm, and introduced in 1950. The plant is a reliable producer.

Characteristics Perfect red cherry tomatoes weighing around 1oz (25g) with an excellent traditional tomato flavor.

How to enjoy Eat handfuls as a healthy snack.

Striadel

☀️ **Hybrid, 75 days** One of the Del series raised by Lewis Derby of the Glasshouse Crops Research Institute in England. Bred from 'Gardener's Delight' (opposite), others in the series include the yellow 'Daffodel,' pink 'Rosadel,' and pale yellowish 'Albadel.'

Characteristics Red cherries with the same sweet tangy flavor as their parent.

How to enjoy Eat in a colorful salad.

Skins faintly striped gold

Velvet Red

☀️ **Heirloom, 78 days** Thought to be synonymous with 'Angora Super Sweet,' this is one of a few plants that has beautiful silvery foliage, which deters pests.

Characteristics Noted for the silver hairs on the leaves and the slightly fuzzy fruits, which taste very sweet.

How to enjoy Eat straight off the vine while you are stroking the leaves.

Fine hairs on stalk

Sparsely hairy fruits

Micro-Tom

☀️ **Heirloom, 65 days** Developed by Scott and Harbaugh at the University of Florida who have also released the yellow fruited 'Micro-Gold.' Particularly tiny plants, ideal for planting in a pot on a windowsill.

Characteristics Miniature, red fruits with a firm texture and sweet taste.

How to enjoy Best eaten freshly picked from the plant.

Jasper

▽ ☼ ☀ **F1 hybrid, 68 days** These semi-bush plants produce high yields of firm fruits and show good disease resistance and heat tolerance.

Characteristics Traditional red cherries in appearance, these fruits have quite a distinctive acidic taste.

How to enjoy Ideal with mozzarella in salads.

Balconi Red

◯ ☀ **Hybrid, 70 days** Small bushy plants bred by Saatzucht Quedlingburg of Germany. They produce trailing stems and therefore are ideal for growing in baskets or window boxes.

Characteristics Small, sweet cherry tomatoes.

How to enjoy Grow with the yellow variety (below) and enjoy the contrasting colors.

Balconi Yellow

◯ ☀ **Hybrid, 70 days** The yellow-fruited version of this popular German variety is an ideal companion for creating colorful containers on a balcony or patio.

Characteristics Very sweet, bright yellow cherry tomatoes.

How to enjoy Use with the red variety (above) for colorful salads.

Decorative, brightly colored fruits

Suncherry Premium

🌱 ☀️ **F1 hybrid, 75 days** An early ripening prolific plant bred in Japan. 'Suncherry Extra Sweet' is part of the same series.

Characteristics These uniform, red tomatoes have very glossy skins and a particularly good sweet flavor.

How to enjoy Use with 'Sungold' (p41) in colorful quiches and flans.

Brown Berry

🌱 ☀️ **Heirloom, 75 days** Bred by Sahin Seeds of The Netherlands, this plant produces a high yield of attractive tomatoes with an unusual color.

Characteristics These distinctive brown tomatoes are not as sweet as those of 'Black Cherry' (p38) or 'Snowberry' (p40).

How to enjoy Best served in a rainbow salad with cherry tomatoes of varying color.

Very juicy fruits

Pepe

🌱 ☀️ **F1 hybrid, 68 days** Very productive plants from the European division of the Japanese Takii Seed Company, with 35–50 fruits in a cluster. High disease resistance.

Characteristics Mid-sized cherry tomatoes with a very sweet taste.

How to enjoy Perfect for nibbling straight off the vine.

Extra Sweetie

🌱 ☀ **F1 hybrid, 70 days** Excellent variety similar to 'Sweet 100' and 'Sweetie,' it produces grapelike clusters of fruits.

Characteristics Bright red tomatoes of an intermediate mini-cherry/grape shape. They have a particularly high sugar content.

How to enjoy Use in children's packed lunches as an easy way to encourage them to eat fruit.

Maskotka

○ ◐ ☀ **Hybrid, 70 days** Compact plants from Poland, the name means "mascot." Ideal for growing in containers, as the tomatoes will tumble over the edge.

Characteristics The sweet fruits weigh 1–1½oz (25–35g) and show good split resistance.

How to enjoy Why not use to make a tasty sauce to accompany Polish golabki—stuffed cabbage rolls?

Particularly juicy fruits

Tomatoberry

🌱 ☀ **F1 hybrid, 60 days** This variety was introduced in 2007 by the Japanese Tokita Seed Company who also released the very popular 'Sungold' (p41).

Characteristics The bright red fruits are shaped like strawberries, giving them a distinctive look, and just like strawberries, they are particularly sweet and juicy.

How to enjoy Eat as a snack or use in a soup.

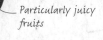

Strawberry-shaped fruits

Green Tiger

☀ Hybrid, 72 days A recent open-pollinated variety, sold throughout supermarkets in the UK.

Characteristics Attractive deep burgundy-colored fruits with olive-green stripes. The glossy skins are thick and resistant to splitting.

How to enjoy Best roasted, because they are too tough for eating raw.

Deep green stripes on skin

Vivid green seeds

Golden Pearl

☀ Heirloom, 60 days This plant produces grapelike clusters of miniature yellow fruits over a long season.

Characteristics The golden-yellow, pea-sized tomatoes have little flesh but large seeds for the size of the fruits.

How to enjoy Best served scattered over a savory dish for their ornamental value.

Picolino

☀ F1 hybrid, 70 days A short-growing but vigorous plant from Holland. Commercially, at least two flowers per truss are removed so the remaining fruits develop as uniformly as possible.

Characteristics Cocktail-type tomato with firm, glossy red fruits averaging 1¼oz (30g) each.

How to enjoy They can seem a little too firm to eat fresh, but are tasty roasted.

Red Pigmy

☼ ☀ **Heirloom, 65 days** This early fruiting variety was introduced by K. Sahin in Holland. Plants grow up to 14in (35cm) tall with a trailing habit ideal for hanging baskets. Unusual leaves have a bumpy surface.

Characteristics Bright red cherry tomatoes sometimes have a yellow tint near the stalk.

How to enjoy Serve in salads with the yellow variety (below) for contrast.

Sometimes have a yellow tint around stalk

Yellow Pigmy

☼ ☀ **Hybrid, 65 days** Released by Sahin Seeds in Holland as a sister variety to the popular 'Red Pigmy' (above).

Characteristics Bright yellow cherry tomatoes. Like other yellow sister varieties, they are slightly sweeter then their red counterpart.

How to enjoy The small, sweet fruits are best eaten whole in salads.

Ruby

🌱 ☀ ☀ **F1 hybrid, 60 days** Vigorous plant from Taiwan produces many long trusses, which each have 25–30 tomatoes. More blight resistant than many varieties.

Characteristics Red fruits, which have a very rich flavor and a particularly sweet and succulent taste.

How to enjoy Perfect for adding color and flavor to Greek salads or try in a soup.

Tumbling Tom Red

▽ ☼ **Hybrid, 78 days** Introduced in England in 2002 by Floranova, these high-yielding plants have a cascading growth habit, making them ideal for containers.

Characteristics Small, sweet, red tomatoes.

How to enjoy Use with 'Tumbling Tom Yellow' (below) and 'Green Grape' to make a "traffic light" salad.

Tumbling Tom Yellow

▽ ☼ **Hybrid, 78 days** The sister to 'Tumbling Tom Red' (above) with the same cascading habit and productivity. Grow in hanging baskets or raised beds on a patio.

Characteristics Small, sweet, yellow tomatoes.

How to enjoy Snack off the bush as you tend to your plants.

Riesentraube

▮ ☼ ☼ **Heirloom, 80 days** Roughly translated as "bunch of grapes," this German variety, widely grown in Pennsylvania in the nineteenth century, was made popular by Curtis D. Choplin of South Carolina in the 1990s.

Characteristics Huge bunches of red tomatoes with pointed ends. Excellent flavor.

How to enjoy Usually eaten fresh in salads, but used traditionally to make tomato wine.

Nipple-shaped pointed ends

Piccolo

F1 hybrid, 78 days Registered in 2007 by the French seed company Gautier Semences, these sprawling plants are easily grown and very disease resistant.

Characteristics Extremely tasty, these tiny, bright red tomatoes are very popular for their intense sweet taste.

How to enjoy Eat them quickly from the vine, before anyone else beats you to them.

Cherrola

F1 hybrid, 72 days Productive plant with long trusses of up to 20 well-spaced fruits. Highly praised in field trials, this variety will be available in seed catalogs from 2009 onward.

Characteristics Produces ornamental clusters of bright red cherries with an excellent flavor.

How to enjoy Use whole in flans and quiches. They are great combined with goat cheese.

Amoroso

F1 hybrid, 72 days A cocktail-type, popular commercial variety from Rijk Zwaan of The Netherlands. Compact plants, which show good disease resistance, produce evenly spaced trusses of fruits.

Characteristics Shiny red fruits have a high sugar content.

How to enjoy Roast whole with other Mediterranean-style vegetables.

Large cherries

Sweet Pea

🌱 ☀️ **Heirloom, 78 days** This prolific currant tomato was produced in Holland. The plants have delicate foliage and produce hundreds of pretty red fruits for harvesting on the vine.

Characteristics Tiny, currant-sized tomatoes weighing just ¹⁄₁₆oz (2g) each have a rich flavor.

How to enjoy Tasty, decorative fruits make jewel-like additions to salads.

Tiny, seedy fruits ——

Broad Ripple Yellow Currant

🌱 ☀️ ☀️ **Heirloom, 75 days** Saved from a plant that was found growing in a pavement crack in the Broad Ripple district of Indianapolis.

Characteristics Prolific producer of small, sweet, low-acid, yellow tomatoes weighing less than ½oz (8–10g) each.

How to enjoy Perfect for children to eat off the vine like sweets.

Gold Rush

🌱 ☀️ **Heirloom, 78 days** Like its sister, 'Sweet Pea' (above), this prolific currant tomato was also produced in Holland. Harvest as a whole truss.

Characteristics The tiny but particularly richly flavored, sweet orange berries stay on the vine for prolonged periods without splitting.

How to enjoy Very decorative, tasty fruits, ideal for garnishing sweet or savory dishes.

Very small fruits

Beefsteak

Beefsteak is probably the most commonly used word to describe large tomatoes that usually have five or more locules. The tomatoes typically weigh 6–9oz (180–250g), but may be huge, weighing more than 2.2lb (1kg). They usually have a slightly flattened look, being wider than they are long, and may seem misshapen. There are a number of varieties, however, that have beautifully fluted outlines. Their meaty flesh makes them ideal for slicing and eating in sandwiches.

Country Taste

⚑ ☼ **F1 hybrid, 78 days** One of relatively few hybrid beefsteak varieties, 'Country Taste' is from the Dutch firm Nunhems Zaden. Shows good resistance to disease.

Characteristics These are meaty, deep red fruits with a good flavor.

How to enjoy Excellent slicing variety for enjoying with burgers and a convenient size for general culinary use.

Dr. Wyche's Yellow

⚑ ☼ **Heirloom, 85 days** Dentist Dr. John Wyche of Cherokee heritage, was part owner of a circus. He used elephant manure to fertilize his Oklahoma tomato garden.

Characteristics Large, deep golden-yellow fruits with a rich flavor and meaty texture.

How to enjoy A lovely variety to slice and serve in sandwiches or makes a well-flavored yellow sauce to serve with fish.

Meaty flesh with few seeds

Pineapple (Ananas)

🌱 ☀️ **Heirloom, 85 days** This potato-leafed plant is a popular heritage variety that comes from Kentucky.

Characteristics The yellow fruits blush red as they ripen and can reach 2.2lb (1kg) in weight. They have a mild, fruity flavor.

How to enjoy The firm flesh is sweet and delicious served simply in wedges with cucumber and melon.

Sometimes has red blush

Aunt Ruby's German Green

🌱 ☀️ ☀️ **Heirloom, 80 days** Ruby Arnold of Greenville, Tennessee, obtained the seed of this tomato from her German grandfather. Be sure to isolate the plant if you are saving seeds.

Characteristics Spicy-sweet, large fruits, weighing 14oz (400g) remain green when ripe.

How to enjoy Best served fresh rather than cooked to appreciate the unusual taste.

Hillbilly Potato Leaf

🌱 ☀️ **Heirloom, 85 days** A late-season gourmet variety from Ohio. The potato-leafed plants are particularly vigorous.

Characteristics The sweet fruits ripen to a mottled-golden color streaked with red, and can reach around 2.2lb (1kg).

How to enjoy The well-flavored fruits are best served fresh in thick slices.

Attractive-patterned flesh

Cuostralée

⚑ ☀ **Heirloom, 85 days** Huge plants produce equally impressive fruits of this popular French variety. In wet summers, grow under cover, as they can be particularly susceptible to foliage diseases (p116).

Characteristics The red, intensely flavored tomatoes can weigh up to 2–3lb (1–1.5kg).

How to enjoy Each tomato could be a meal in itself, but are best shared with friends.

Many seed chambers

Faworyt

⚑ ☀ ☀ **Hybrid, 70 days** Meaning "favorite" in Polish, these compact-growing plants were raised by PlantiCo of Poland. They perform well in various growing conditions.

Characteristics These large, sweet fruits of around 14oz (400g) are a raspberry-pink color.

How to enjoy Delicious sweet-fleshed variety to be savored fresh.

Few seeds

Halladay's Mortgage Lifter

⚑ ☀ **Heirloom, 90 days** Marshall Cletis Byles sold his own strain of this variety, 'Radiator Charlie's Mortgage Lifter,' to pay off his mortgage. This strain comes from relatives of James Halladay of Pennsylvania.

Characteristics These usually weigh 14oz–1¾lb (400–800g), and are resistant to splitting.

How to enjoy Savor in slices or sell to pay off your own mortgage.

Legend

☰ ☀ ☀ **Hybrid, 68 days** Bred by Baggett and Myers at Oregon State University. Sets earlier fruit than the related 'Oregon Spring.' Excellent for cool climates and notable for its blight resistance.

Characteristics Variable-sized fruits that may exceed 14oz (400g), with few seeds.

How to enjoy Delicious grilled with a drizzle of olive oil.

Ananas Noir

🌱 ☀ **Heirloom, 85 days** Translated as "black pineapple," this high-yielding French plant introduced in 2005 by Pascal Moreau won't always come true from seed.

Characteristics These large, multicolored fruits can weigh around 20oz (600g). They have a rich taste described as smoky with citrus hints.

How to enjoy To appreciate the rainbow of colors and distinct flavor, serve in salads.

Green, red, and yellow flesh

Pink Accordion

🌱 ☀ ☀ **Heirloom, 78 days** Very popular heritage variety, admired for the unusual shape of the tomatoes.

Characteristics The large, pinkish red fruits are ruffled like an accordion. They have a mild, sweet flavor.

How to enjoy Fruits are easy to hollow out and look beautiful stuffed.

Hollow fruits

Jack Hawkins

🌱 ☀️ **Hybrid, 72 days** A commercial variety bred in the US, these plants are much grown for the supermarket trade.

Characteristics The large, well-flavored fruits have a particularly sweet flesh.

How to enjoy Slice to serve on burgers or use to make a wonderful soup.

Pantano

🌱 ☀️ **Heirloom, 70 days** *Pantano* is Italian for "marsh" and this productive variety, also known as 'Pantano Romanesco,' is said to have been grown on the former marshes near Rome.

Characteristics These large, scalloped fruits are usually green around the shoulders.

How to enjoy The thick, tasty flesh and few seeds make this an excellent slicing tomato.

Costoluto Genovese

🌱 ☀️ ☀️ **Heirloom, 78 days** *Costoluto* means "ribbed" in Italian and these big, beautifully ruffled tomatoes were one of the first kinds of tomatoes to be introduced to Europe in the sixteenth century.

Characteristics These attractive, scalloped, cherry-red fruits have a firm, meaty texture.

How to enjoy Traditionally used in Italy for purées, they are ideal for juicing too.

Ribbed fruits —

Costoluto Fiorentino

☀ ☀ **Heirloom, 80 days** A variety from Tuscany in Italy, closely related to but usually not as ruffled as 'Costoluto Genovese' (opposite).

Characteristics These juicy, bright red fruits are variable in shape, usually slightly ribbed.

How to enjoy Wonderful on pizzas or use to make flavorful risottos and to add a meaty component to salads.

Attractive-patterned flesh

Amana Orange

☀ **Heirloom, 80 days** Introduced in 1985 by Gary Staley of Florida, who named it after the Amana Corporation where he worked as a customer service manager.

Characteristics Big and beautiful, the shiny orange, ribbed fruits have a mild taste.

How to enjoy Admire sliced thinly on a plate, sprinkled with torn basil leaves.

Solid flesh with few seeds

Delicious

☀ **Heirloom, 78 days** Introduced by Burpee Seeds in the US in 1964. This variety holds the Guinness World Record for the heaviest tomato ever grown.

Characteristics Fruits average 1.7lb (800g). They can be very sweet, but sadly the biggest fruits do not necessarily live up to their name.

How to enjoy Use for soups and sauces or to make an attempt on that world record (p126).

Big Boy

☀ ☀ **F1 hybrid, 78 days** Bred by
Oved Shifriss and released in 1949 by
Burpee Seeds in the US, 'Big Boy' is a much-
loved variety still in production as an F1
hybrid. Others in the series, including 'Ultra
Boy,' 'Ultra Girl,' and 'Early Girl,' show better
disease resistance.

Characteristics Large, bright red fruits.

How to enjoy Use to make excellent ketchup.

Better Boy

☀ ☀ **F1 hybrid, 72 days** Improved
version of 'Big Boy' (above) the plant has
greater disease resistance and productivity.
The plant holds the world record for the
most tomatoes produced by a single plant,
at 340lb (155kg).

Characteristics Large, evenly shaped fruits.

How to enjoy Perfect for slicing in sandwiches.

Blue Ridge Mountain

☀ **Heirloom, 82 days** A potato-leafed
plant from the Blue Ridge Mountain region
of North Carolina.

Characteristics Well-flavored sweet fruits are
pinkish red and weigh around 20oz (600g).

How to enjoy Ideal for sauces and salsas.

*Richly colored fruits
with a pink tinge*

Supermarmande

⩔ ☀ **Heirloom, 62 days** 'Marmande,' named after the area of France from where the variety came, is a very popular old semi-bush plant. 'Supermarmande' crops earlier and shows more disease resistance. 'Rouge de Marmande' (Burkes Backyard) is popular in Australia.

Characteristics Large, flavorsome fruits.

How to enjoy Use in soups, salads, and coulis.

Lightly-ribbed, cherry-red fruits

Brandywine

🌱 ☀ **Heirloom, 85 days** Introduced in 1889, this extremely popular tomato was named after the Brandywine River in Pennsylvania. Originally blood red, there are now many strains of different colors.

Characteristics These large fruits (shown here enlarged but not in proportion) in the 14oz–1.7lb (400–800g) range have a characteristic sweet taste.

How to enjoy Wonderful served fresh in slices.

Often cracks at shoulders

Dense flesh

Evergreen

❦ ☀ **Heirloom, 75 days** Introduced by Glecklers Seedmen of Ohio in 1956, this variety is also called 'Emerald Evergreen' and 'Tasty Evergreen'.

Characteristics Easily peeled, greenish yellow fruits that have a lovely citruslike flavor.

How to enjoy Excellent when used half-and-half with apples in open tarts.

Purple Calabash

❦ ☀ ☀ **Heirloom, 85 days** Originating in Texas, 'Purple Calabash' was first released commercially in 1987 by Glecklers Seedmen and others.

Characteristics A most unusual heavily ribbed tomato that is an intriguing rich purplish red color like a well-ripened loganberry. Has a tangy and somewhat spicy flavor.

How to enjoy Best used in casseroles.

Deeply ruffled fruits

Kellogg's Breakfast

❦ ☀ **Heirloom, 79 days** Named after Darrell Kellogg of Michigan, not the purveyor of breakfast cereals, this is a popular and prolific plant.

Characteristics These large, vibrant orange fruits are somewhat irregular in shape and have thin skins.

How to enjoy Use to make rich-flavored and brightly colored juices.

Vibrant orange fruits

German Pink

☼ ☀ **Heirloom, 85 days** A potato-leafed plant taken to America in 1883 from Bremen, Germany, by Michael Ott.

Characteristics The large, pinkish red fruits weigh over 14oz (400g) and contain few seeds.

How to enjoy The fruits are traditionally eaten in slices, sprinkled with sugar. Alternatively, enjoy in a salad.

Meaty flesh with few seeds

Black Russian

☼ ☀ ☀ **Heirloom, 78 days** A mid-season variety from Russia. Popular in Australia, because it copes well with the climate.

Characteristics These deep maroon-colored fruits often remain green at the shoulders. Good tender flesh, but the fruits can be prone to splitting.

How to enjoy Include sliced in a salad with red and green varieties for color contrast.

Often remains green at shoulders

Rose de Berne

☼ ☀ **Heirloom, 75 days** Attractive rosy-pink tomato from Switzerland. The name translates as "rose from Berne," Switzerland's capital.

Characteristics Variable in shape and size from 5–7oz (150–200g), but always with an intense sweet taste and a low acid content.

How to enjoy Serve in thick slices with cheese or cold meats.

Soft, meaty flesh

Thin skin

Gold Medal

🌱 ☀ **Heirloom, 85 days** Introduced in the US as 'Ruby Gold' by John Lewis Childs in 1921, this variety has had several name changes and was also called 'Early Sunrise'.

Characteristics The large, sweet fruits (shown here enlarged but not in proportion) are orange-yellow streaked throughout with red.

How to enjoy Eat fresh or use to make a wonderful refreshing juice.

Orange flesh streaked with red

Sweet and particularly soft flesh

Aker's West Virginia

🌱 ☀ **Heirloom, 88 days** A family heirloom from Carl Aker of West Virginia, home to many other heritage varieties including the pink-fruited 'Tappy's Finest' and 'West Virginia Straw.' Plants are high yielding and disease resistant.

Characteristics Large fruits with a rich flavor.

How to enjoy Excellent for slicing.

May show concentric cracks around stalk

Big Rainbow

🍴 ☀️ **Heirloom, 85 days** Named by Dorothy Beiswenger of Minnesota in 1983, this is a huge red and yellow tomato. It certainly lives up to its name. In cool climates, grow under glass.

Characteristics These large, colorful, meaty fruits average around 20oz (600g).

How to enjoy A delightful, well-flavored tomato for eating fresh or making great salsas.

Few seeds

Streaked red and yellow flesh

Black Krim

🍴 ☀️ ☀️ **Heirloom, 75 days** Also known as 'Czerno Krimski' or 'Black Crimean,' this tomato comes from the south of Ukraine.

Characteristics The richly colored fruits have a soft texture and an intense flavor, sometimes described as smoky. Fruits can be prone to cracking.

How to enjoy The large fruits are wonderful grilled and served with bacon for breakfast.

Rich mahogany-colored skin

Cherokee Purple

🍴 ☀️ **Heirloom, 80 days** Popular heritage variety distributed by John D. Green of Tennessee, whose source said her ancestors obtained it from the local Cherokee people. Shows some blight tolerance.

Characteristics These dusky-maroon fruits stay green at the shoulders and vary from 5 to 14oz (150 to 400g). The flesh has a sweet intensity.

How to enjoy Eat fresh as you would an apple.

Plum

Plum tomatoes have an elongated, oblong shape, and are typically 3–3½in (7–9cm) long and 1½–2in (4–5cm) in diameter. Use these for making sauces and purées—their flesh has a higher solid content than most other tomatoes, which gives great flavor and texture. They are particularly known for their use in canning. Mini-plum varieties have a thicker flesh than cherry tomatoes, and are equally good for snacking. They are ideal for packing in lunchboxes, as they won't bruise easily.

Olivade

🌱 ☀ F1 Hybrid, 72 days Excellent, productive plants suitable for greenhouse or outdoors, yielding around 60 fruits per plant. Shows good disease resistance.

Characteristics Large plum fruits averaging 4oz (100g) with deep red skin and juicy flesh. A good long-keeping variety with few seeds.

How to enjoy In richly flavored sauces to eat with pasta.

Black Plum

🌱 ☀ ☀ Heirloom, 82 days This plant from Russia crops well even in cooler climates. Plants may be grown as semi-bushes.

Characteristics The firm-textured, purplish red fruits are an appealing even plum shape and are very juicy.

How to enjoy A crisp-textured tomato for snacking or equally good roasted in olive oil.

Deep red skins

Juicy flesh

Deeper color at shoulders

San Marzano Lungo

¶ ☀ **F1 Hybrid, 75 days** A popular strain of the well-known Italian plum tomato, which also has miniature and pink variants. Crops consistently over a long period.

Characteristics Elongated plum fruits with a dry, mealy texture.

How to enjoy Use in sauces, soups, and tomato paste; also excellent for drying.

Stubby ends

Roma

✾ ☀ **Heirloom, 78 days** Compact bush bred by the United States Department of Agriculture in 1955. Later selections have improved disease resistance.

Characteristics Looks like a traditional Italian plum tomato in shape and color. Good taste with solid, meaty flesh.

How to enjoy Specifically bred for canning, but suitable for most cooking purposes.

Rio Grande

✾ ☼ ☼ ☀ **Heirloom, 80 days** Productive semi-bush plants show good disease resistance and tolerance of extreme temperatures. Widely grown in Greece.

Characteristics Fairly blocklike, plum-shaped fruits that are a deep red color.

How to enjoy Ideal for sauces and making fresh tomato juice. Grown commercially in Turkey for sun-dried tomatoes.

Pointed tip

Principe Borghese

☗ ☀ **Heirloom, 75 days** Italian heritage variety known by 1911. Although a bush plant, it needs to be staked due to the weight of fruits produced.

Characteristics Heavy clusters of small plum-shaped fruits. A good long-keeping variety with few seeds.

How to enjoy Can be enjoyed in soups and sauces, but is best used for drying.

Few seeds

Alaskan Fancy

☗ ☀ ☀ **Heirloom, 55 days** An early and reliable cropper. It was bred for the cool climate and short growing season of Alaska. Performs well in poor summers.

Characteristics These medium-sized, juicy red tomatoes have a good flavor compared to many other plum varieties.

How to enjoy Great for salads, but flavor improves when cooked for sauces and soups.

Aviro

☗ ☀ ☀ **F1 hybrid, 70 days** Formerly known as 'Orange Plum,' this productive plant shows good virus resistance.

Characteristics These medium-sized, pointed plums are orange-scarlet in color and, like other orange varieties, have particularly high beta-carotene and vitamin C levels.

How to enjoy Pretty fruits to include in salads, or are also excellent roasted.

Long Tom

☀ ✱ **Heirloom, 85 days** 'Long Tom' originated in Pennsylvania, but is closely related to the elongated Italian plums.

Characteristics These deep red plums have a good flavor and little juice.

How to enjoy The low acidity and firm texture make this variety excellent on sandwiches. Also a good choice for infusing flavour into sauces and soups.

Blondköpfchen

☀ ✱ ✱ **Heirloom, 78 days** Translated as "little blonde girl," this very productive German plant yields huge trusses of long-lasting fruits.

Characteristics These small, golden-yellow baby plum-shaped fruits are sweet and resistant to splitting.

How to enjoy One of the best mini-plum varieties for roasting whole.

Jersey Giant

☀ ✱ **Heirloom, 85 days** Like the chicken of this name, the Jersey Giant tomato is from New Jersey.

Particularly large fruits

Characteristics Large, elongated plum-shaped tomatoes with firm, sweet flesh and few seeds.

How to enjoy One of the best varieties for making tomato paste.

Purple Russian

🌱 ☼ ☀ **Heirloom, 80 days** High-yielding plants from the Ukraine.

Characteristics Violet-colored plums averaging around 5oz (150g) with a firm texture and excellent flavor. They keep well.

How to enjoy Attractive sliced in salads, or will dry well for winter use.

Many seed chambers

Speckled Roman

🌱 ☼ **Heirloom, 85 days** The result of a cross between 'Banana Legs' and 'Antique Roman' that took place in the Illinois garden of John F. Swenson. It is similar to 'Casady's Folly' and 'Opalka.'

Characteristics Beautifully pointed plums with stripes and speckles and a firm, meaty flesh.

How to enjoy Enjoy as a work of art before halving and roasting.

Unusual striped skin

Yellow Butterfly

🌱 ☼ **Heirloom, 68 days** A prolific producer of mini-plum tomatoes similar to 'Ildi' (p73), this plant is becoming more widely grown. Rampant plants produce an extraordinary number of fruits in a truss.

Characteristics These ornamental, dainty fruits have a pleasant sweet taste.

How to enjoy Cut trusses of tomatoes and hang indoors. Nibble at your leisure.

Plum- or pear-shaped fruits

Golden Sweet

F1 hybrid, 65 days Mini-plum hybrid from Taiwan that produces clusters of around 40 pretty yellow plum-cherry tomatoes.

Characteristics Tomatoes resemble oversized grapes and have a mild, sweet flavor and firm texture. Resistant to splitting.

How to enjoy Ideal nibbling fruits for lunchboxes and picnics or use in sweet pickles.

Juliet

F1 hybrid, 60 days A mini-plum-shaped variety developed in Taiwan, sister to the well-known 'Santa' (below).

Characteristics A thick skin that is resistant to splitting makes 'Juliet' a very popular commercial tomato.

How to enjoy Lovely in Mediterranean-style casseroles, but the thick skin means they are a little chewy when eaten fresh.

Deep red fruits

Yellow Santa

F1 hybrid, 70 days Bred by the Known-You Seed Company of Taiwan, the 'Santa' mini-plum variety is very popular with commercial growers. A number of similar varieties including this yellow form have now been released.

Characteristics Very sweet, glossy fruits with a tough skin, so they store well.

How to enjoy An ideal snacking tomato.

Rosada

☂ ☀ **F1 hybrid, 75 days** A high-yielding plum-cherry hybrid from Taiwan that is sadly susceptible to splitting. Often favored in a taste trials.

Characteristics The bright red mini-plums have a great depth of flavor.

How to enjoy These thin-skinned fruits are best eaten straight from the vine or used to flavour soups.

Floridity

☂ ☀ **F1 hybrid, 62 days** These plants, from the English firm Tozer Seeds, produce many fruits over a long-cropping season. Voted top in a UK taste test in 2007.

Characteristics These mini-plum-shaped tomatoes are resistant to splitting.

How to enjoy Ideal for nibbling straight from the vine and making soups and sauces.

Rudolph

☂ ☀ **F1 hybrid, 68 days** Like its sister variety 'Santa' (p69), this was bred by the Known-You Seed Company of Taiwan. It produces long trusses of up to 25 fruits.

Characteristics Mid-sized plums with a firm texture and excellent flavor.

How to enjoy Halve and bake in the oven, or are a good choice for making soups or drying.

Firm fruits ——

—— *Few seeds*

Old Ivory Egg

🌱 ☼ ☼ **Heirloom, 75 days** This Australian variety, also known as 'Ivory Egg' and 'Australian Yellow Plum,' was listed by the American Seed Savers Exchange in 1985.

Characteristics Sweet, citrusy, plum-shaped fruits that are around the size of a small hen's egg.

How to enjoy Best eaten raw in salads, as the flesh tends to disintegrate on cooking.

Creamy yellow when fully ripe

Mini-Charm

🌱 ☼ **F1 hybrid, 75 days** Hybrid plant from the US, which shows good resistance to disease. Vigorous plants with well-spaced-out leaves.

Characteristics Mini-plum-shaped, red fruits, just ¼oz (10g) each, are very juicy.

How to enjoy Tiny tomatoes with a very sweet flavor, they are ideal for lunchboxes.

Dasher

🌱 ☼ **F1 hybrid, 65 days** A mini-plum tomato grown commercially in Italy. Plants are sometimes offered to gardeners as grafted transplants.

Characteristics Appealing red mini-plums that are known for their excellent sweet flavor.

How to enjoy Straight off the vine as the ideal nibbling snack.

Orange Banana

🌱 ☼ ☀ **Heirloom, 80 days** A high-yielding Russian heirloom that can be grown under cover or outdoors.

Characteristics These deep orange fruits are plum shaped with a pointed nipple-like tip.

How to enjoy The richly flavored fruits make a wonderful golden sauce or are good for drying to use in the winter.

Often remains green at shoulders

Cornue des Andes

🌱 ☼ ☀ **Heirloom, 78 days** Collected in the Andes by a French seed collector, other names for this variety include 'Des Andes,' 'Andine Cornue,' and 'Poivron des Andes.' Plants can be prone to mildew.

Characteristics Elongated plum-, pimento-, or horn-shaped red fruits with pointed tips.

How to enjoy Their strong flavor is excellent in chutneys and ketchups.

Easily removable skin

Some have curved tip

Few seeds

Sunstream

🌱 ☼ **F1 hybrid, 72 days** Popular new hybrid from the Dutch firm Enza Zaden that shows good disease resistance.

Characteristics These blocklike fruits with glossy red skins have an excellent flavor.

How to enjoy Halve and roast these fruits with olive oil or use for drying.

Apero

✂ ☼ **F1 hybrid, 65 days** Winner of the
tastiest tomato competition at West Dean,
England in 2008, this British tomato is
produced on many compact trusses.

Characteristics These glossy red fruits are
renowned for their great flavor.

How to enjoy Pop them straight in your
mouth to appreciate their succulent taste.

Chiquita

∀ ☼ **F1 hybrid, 63 days** Low-growing
bushy plants are excellent for growing in
pots and hanging baskets.

Characteristics These dusky pink baby plums
have a firm flesh and superb flavor.

How to enjoy Add to a fresh fruit salad for
an interesting dessert.

*Dusky pink
in color*

Ildi

✂ ☼ **Hybrid, 70 days** From the German
firm Saatzucht Quedlingburg, 'Ildi' is a
diminutive of the Hungarian girl's name
Ildikó. Plants produce trusses of up to 80
fruits with a total of around 700 per plant.

Characteristics Mini-plum/pear-shaped fruits.

How to enjoy Hang trusses in a cool place and
they will keep for weeks. The dainty fruits look
pretty in an edible floral arrangement.

Weird and wonderful

Many tomatoes do not easily fit into any of the main categories. For example, there are a number of extreme variations of the plum shape—banana-, carrot-, sausage-, and flask-shaped fruits all appear. Pear-shaped variants with a distinct bottle neck are often considered a gourmet fruit. Oxheart varieties, which look like giant strawberries, often have a dense flesh and a delicious flavor. And blocky, squarish-shaped hollow fruits resembling bell peppers are ideal for stuffing.

Yellow Stuffer

❦ ☼ **Heirloom, 85 days** Also known as 'Gourmet Yellow Stuffer' or 'Yellow Cup,' this variety was bred in the 1980s by Colen Wyatt of Petoseed in the US.

Characteristics The deep yellow fruits are the shape of a bell pepper with thick walls and a hollow interior.

How to enjoy Stuff with a savory filling of your choice, such as risotto or lentils.

Hollow cavities inside

Yellow Pear

❦ ☼ ☼ **Heirloom, 75 days** Also known as 'Beam's Yellow Pear,' this is a very old variety that may date back as far as the seventeenth century. Vigorous plants produce fruits over a long season.

Characteristics These baby pear-shaped fruits with a sweet taste weigh around ½oz (15g).

How to enjoy These tasty fruits look very appealing in salads or to eat by the handful.

Distinct bottle neck

Red Fig

🌱 ☀ **Heirloom, 85 days** This American variety from the eighteenth century is closely related to 'Red Pear.' It was traditionally dried for use in the winter as a fig substitute. The plant crops heavily.

Characteristics Small pear-shaped, juicy fruits.

How to enjoy Attractive fruits are good to eat fresh, but would traditionally be sun-dried.

Japanese Black Trifele

🌱 ☀ ☀ ☀ **Heirloom, 80 days** Despite its name, this variety, also known as 'Yaponskiy Trufel,' is thought to be of Estonian origin.

Split-resistant skins

Characteristics These fascinating fruits vary greatly, but can be the size and shape of a large pear, richly colored in red-maroon.

How to enjoy Eat cut into thick wedges to appreciate the wonderful, rich flavor.

Plum Lemon

🌱 ☀ ☀ **Heirloom, 81 days** A vigorous, disease-resistant plant originating in St. Petersburg, Russia. It was introduced to the US in 1991 by Kent Whealy, who received it from a Moscow seedsman.

May ripen to a golden-yellow color

Characteristics The fruits are usually somewhat lemonlike in both shape and color.

How to enjoy The firm, meaty tomatoes have a mild, vaguely citrus taste, best eaten fresh.

Yellow Oxheart

⚘ ☀ **Heirloom, 80 days** A family heirloom from Virginia that is thought to date back to around 1915. The finely divided leaves can show poor resistance to disease.

Characteristics The medium to large heart-shaped fruits are light yellow in color and have good, juicy flesh.

How to enjoy The succulence and excellent flavor of this tomato make it ideal for juicing.

Cuor di Bue

⚘ ☀ **Heirloom, 75 days** Translated as "heart of beef," this Italian oxheart variety is similar to the French 'Coeur de Boeuf.' Lax plants produce very dense, heavy fruits and need to be well-supported.

Characteristics These tomatoes have rich red flesh and few seeds. Fruits usually weigh around 7oz (200g), but can exceed 14oz (400g).

How to enjoy Wonderful in simple salads.

Orange Strawberry

⚘ ☀ **Heirloom, 75 days** Originating in 1993 in the garden of Marjorie Morris of Indiana as a chance seedling from 'Pineapple' (p53), this beautiful orange variety is sometimes late to mature.

Characteristics The strawberry-shaped fruits have a firm, dry flesh that is richly flavored.

How to enjoy Admire the fruits as *objets d'art* before enjoying their strong taste.

Strawberry-shaped fruits

Green Bell Pepper

† ☼ **Heirloom, 75 days** This variety was bred by Thomas P. Wagner of Washington, founder of Tater Mater Seeds, from his 'Brown Derby Mix.'

Characteristics Unusual green-and-yellow-striped, hollow tomato. The flesh is firm, very much like a bell pepper.

How to enjoy Ideal for stuffing with a savory filling or sliced into rings for salads.

Hollow inside

Reisetomate

† ☼ **Heirloom, 65 days** Also known as 'Pocketbook' and 'Voyage,' this variety may be from Austria, but is similar to tomatoes used by native peoples in Central America. Translates from German as "travel tomato."

Characteristics These bizarre fruits resemble bunches of cherry tomatoes stuck together.

How to enjoy Traditionally said to have been eaten by travelers, one piece at a time.

Multilobed fruits, may have many segments

Green Sausage

∀ ☼ **Heirloom, 65 days** Originally raised in the US by Thomas P. Wagner, who called it 'Greensleeves,' this variety was introduced commercially in 1998 by Kees Sahin of Sahin Zaden in The Netherlands.

Characteristics Elongated sausage-shaped fruits that are often curved like a banana.

How to enjoy With its distinctive appearance and taste, this is a tomato to savor fresh.

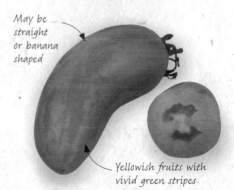

May be straight or banana shaped

Yellowish fruits with vivid green stripes

In the garden

Growing tomatoes in your garden gives you endless pleasure. Firstly, decide on where to grow your plants and whether you want to start from seeds or plantlets. The rituals of plant nurture—watering, feeding, removing sideshoots—are tasks to look forward to every day. Once you've harvested your first successful crop, you'll want to expand your tomato skills—try some grafting, embark on crop rotation, and even create your own variety!

A tomato for every climate

Because tomatoes originated in the coastal highlands of South America, they are not well adapted to extremes of temperature. However, some plants are more suited to some climates than others.

Choosing appropriate tomato plants for your environment will give you a better chance of a successful crop. No tomato plants are able to survive frost, but there are a large number that have been developed to be able to crop successfully in cooler climates. However, if you have your heart set on growing a particular variety, you may be able to adapt the microclimate of your garden to suit it. For example, a variety that prefers warm conditions, such as 'Pink Accordion' (p55), may thrive in cool conditions if set against a sunny wall and sheltered from cold winds.

Strange as it may seem, many cold-tolerant plants are also best for growing in hot climates. That is because they are generally early-fruiting plants; if started at the beginning of the year, they produce a good crop before the intense heat of summer.

Survive the chill

For cold climates, try standard globe varieties 'Glacier,' 'Polar Baby,' 'Siberian' (p34), and 'Sub-Arctic Plenty' (p34); plum varieties 'Alaskan Fancy' and 'Aviro' (p66); and the cherry tomato 'Black Cherry.' The French 'Carmello' is very productive even in cool weather, as is 'Stupice' (p27). 'Scotland Yellow' (p28) is a good, reliable choice.

Black Cherry
(p38)

Glacier
(p23)

Alaskan Fancy
(p66)

Stand the heat

The Florida Agricultural Experiment Station has released many heat-tolerant tomato plants, starting with the popular variety 'Marglobe' in 1925. Others worth trying are standard globe varieties 'Mule Team' (p25), 'Stone,' 'Thessaloniki,' and 'Tropic'; the Italian beefsteaks 'Costoluto Genovese' (p56) and 'Costoluto Fiorentino,' as well as 'Great White,' 'Homestead,' and the ribbed beefsteak 'Pink Accordion' (p55); and plum tomatoes 'Amish Paste' and 'Roma.'

Roma
(p65)

Costoluto Fiorentino
(p57)

Legend
(p55)

Ferline
(p23)

Come with a raincoat

The most important consideration in wet climates is choosing plants that resist fungal diseases, particularly the dreaded late blight (pp114–119). This is caused by the fungus *Phytophthora infestans* and can wipe out an entire crop in wet summers. Large-fruited plants tend to be more susceptible to the disease. Sadly, no tomato plant can be said to be totally blight-immune, but resistant plants worth trying include 'Early Cascade,' 'Fantasio,' 'Ferline,' and 'Legend.'

Where should I grow my tomatoes?

Tomatoes are very adaptable plants and most will grow well in containers, in the ground, as well as under cover. Choose a site where you can appreciate the plants when they come into their full bloom.

Patio pot

Growing tomatoes in pots means they are easy to transport, so you can position them where you like. They prefer a warm, sunny, sheltered position where they will have protection from excessive wind and rain.

Large plants may become too top-heavy for the pot or exhaust the water and nutrient supply in the soil mix too quickly. The smaller bush or dwarf plants are the best choice because they will not impinge on any seating space. Dwarf plants such as 'Balconi Red' (p44), 'Minibel,' and 'Micro-Tom' (p43) should crop successfully even in a 6in (15cm) pot. However, for most other plants, it is a case of bigger is better when it comes to pot size. Terracotta pots look attractive but dry out quickly, alternatively use glazed (or plastic) pots.

Hanging basket

Cherry tomatoes cascading from a hanging basket can be very decorative, as well as productive. Bush plants, such as 'Tumbler' (p36) and 'Tumbling Tom Red' (p49), are easiest to use: they do not need to be pinched off, and naturally trail. Hanging baskets can dry out very quickly, particularly in warm breezes, and may need watering several times a day.

Line the basket with perforated black plastic, use a basket with an integral water reservoir, or put a handful of ice cubes to melt into the basket each morning.

Alternatively, why not grow your tomatoes in a plastic planting pouch? Plant a dwarf, bush, or trailing tomato plant into these soil-filled plastic pouches, hang from the center of a greenhouse or a tree, and watch the colorful cascade emerge.

Growing bag

These sealed plastic bags provide a very popular and fairly cheap method of growing tomatoes, particularly cordon plants such as 'Ailsa Craig' (p32) or 'Gardener's Delight' (p42). They are filled with a proprietary growing medium, usually based on fertilized peat or a peat substitute, but you could try using ordinary bags of soil mix. Many, however, contain just 9 gallons (35 liters) of mix and are very shallow, giving little space for healthy root growth. They can be quite tricky to keep evenly watered, and regular feeding is essential. You could stand bottomless pots on top of the growing bag and fill these with soil mix so that the plant can root to a greater depth (this is called ring culture).

Basket case Position your hanging baskets on a porch so that you can snack on a few tomatoes as you enter or leave the house.

In the bag Cordon tomatoes are ideal for growing bags. Tie canes to greenhouse struts or a trellis to hold them upright.

In the ground

Any type of tomato plant can be grown in open ground. This allows the plants to utilize available water and nutrients from the soil. The plants may also be planted deeply, which encourages them to produce plenty of fibrous, feeding roots. However, depending on the weather and soil fertility, they may still need regular watering and supplementary feeding. In warm climates or in particularly good summers in temperate regions, tomatoes grown outdoors usually produce the most flavorful fruit. It doesn't matter whether the plants are crammed into a flower border (cottage-garden style), in the vegetable garden, or perhaps on an allotment or in a field. Good crops can result from plants in any of these situations. It is, however, important to consider choosing plants that are more resistant to pests and diseases (pp114–119); tomato blight in particular can be a problem with outdoor crops. Some outdoor bush tomatoes may be allowed to sprawl over the ground, but this makes them vulnerable to pests, such as slugs, and to rotting. Support them with canes and twine or proprietary support systems.

Formal potager

Originating in France, potagers are kitchen gardens of fruit and vegetables laid out in decorative patterns, often with geometric beds edged with low box hedges. They usually include flowers and herbs, which are planted among the vegetables to encourage pollinating insects, and for decorative effect. Tomato plants, with their vines of colorful fruits, are great for such gardens. While bush plants tend to be the most popular for outdoor use, they usually produce all their fruits at once, which is not ideal if you want the potager to look decorative for a long season. It may be better to grow cordon plants trained to sturdy stakes. To maximize visual appeal, train the vines up cast-iron obelisks or over garden arches so that the trusses of ripening tomatoes can hang down and catch the light.

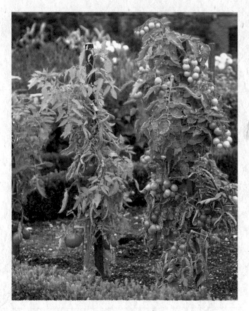

Lean on me Cordon plants need a sturdy support, such as a single stake. You could use horizontal training wires on a warm wall.

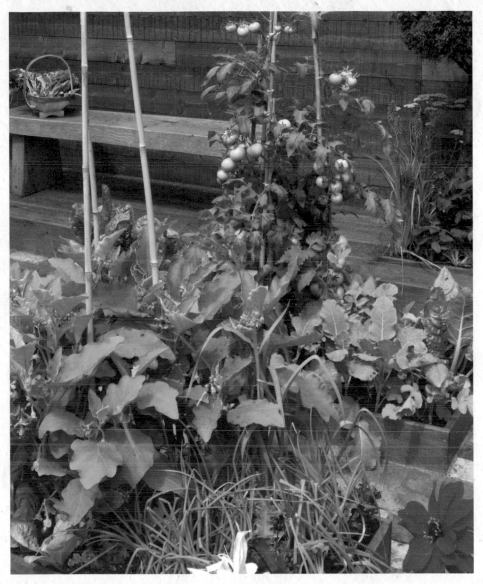

Outdoor kitchen Growing tomatoes with other plants makes an attractive display.

Greenhouses and polytunnels

Growing tomatoes under cover is especially beneficial in climates that have cool, wet summers since it extends the season over which they bear fruit and offers protection from diseases, especially the fungal disease late blight (pp114–119). However, some pests such as whitefly also enjoy life under cover and can be more of a problem in a greenhouse than outdoors.

Polytunnels are usually much cheaper than greenhouses and consist of plastic film stretched over galvanized steel arches to form a walk-in tunnel. They are more susceptible to wind than greenhouses, so must be well-braced with secured arches. The curved shape encloses a larger volume of air than a greenhouse, so a polytunnel stays warmer for longer. Plastic films usually contain ultraviolet light inhibitors and also reduce risk of mildew, rot, and insect attack.

An unheated greenhouse or polytunnel does not give frost protection in temperate regions, but extends the season. Tomato plants will crop all year round with supplementary heating. The limiting factor for plant growth in winter is often lack of light. Orientate the greenhouse east to west to increase light transmission, and clean the glass: clear panes let through nearly 50 percent more light than dirty ones.

Growing tomatoes under cover

You can plant tomatoes directly in soil beds in the greenhouse to give them a greater rooting area. However, growing them in the same beds every year exposes the plants to many soil-borne pests and diseases. Use growing bags or containers to avoid this.

Poor ventilation can lead to very high temperatures on sunny days as well as inadequate air flow, causing high humidity, which may encourage fungal diseases. Automatic window openers and vents are worth investing in. Apply shading to the glass in summer. On hot days, water the floor of the greenhouse to cool the air, but without wetting the tomato foliage.

Window cleaning Keep the glass of your greenhouse clean to allow maximum light transmission to your plants.

Warm up Polytunnels encase more air, so stay warm for longer then greenhouses. **>**

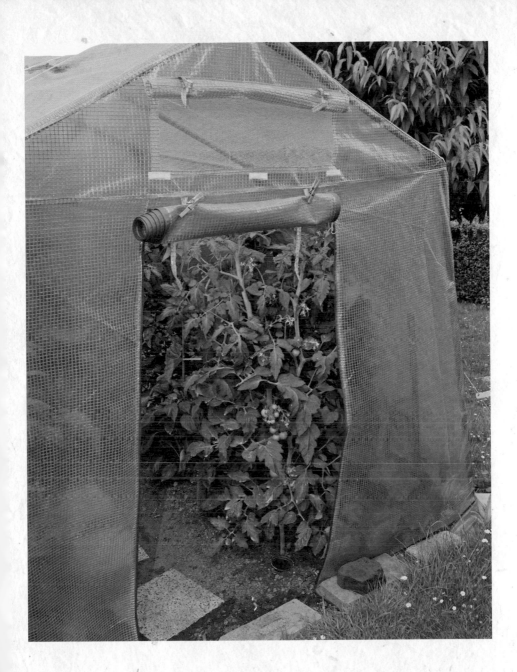

Preparing the soil

Tomatoes are greedy feeders and grow best in a rich, fertile, and moisture-retentive soil. Digging over the soil and incorporating plenty of organic matter will get your plants off to a good start.

Do-it-yourself compost

The best way to improve and enrich soil for tomatoes is to add plenty of organic matter, and homemade compost is an excellent source. Composting utilizes the biochemical process of decomposition, carried out by naturally occurring organisms. Using a compost bin will facilitate the process, but you could build a traditional open heap in a corner of the garden. Open heaps are, however, more likely to have significant weed populations and the resulting compost may contain fewer nutrients because they will have been leached out by rainfall.

A compost heap needs air, moisture, and warmth to keep active, so keep it fairly sheltered, just moist, and aerated. Regularly turning a heap increases oxygen levels and accelerates the process, but is not essential.

MAKING YOUR OWN COMPOST – convert waste into valuable soil conditioner

1 Collect vegetable waste from the kitchen and other soft, green matter from the garden to form the basis of compost.

2 Add the green waste to the bin with drier, fibrous material such as shredded prunings, dead leaves, paper, and cardboard.

Enrich the soil

Late winter or early spring is the best time to prepare the soil for growing tomatoes. As well as homemade compost, you can use other organic materials such as well-rotted manure or composted bark. Clear the bed of any weeds first. If you don't want to disturb the soil structure, you can simply spread a 3in (7.5cm) layer of organic matter on the surface of the soil and let the worms take it in. However, if your homemade compost contains a lot of weed seeds, it is better to dig it in to stop the seeds germinating.

Garden compost makes a great soil conditioner. Use it as potting compost too, if it is reasonably free of weed seeds.

Seed or plantlet?

Watching a seed transform into a plant is a great pleasure. Seeds are cheap and many varieties are readily available. Alternatively, you can cut out the germination period and buy a healthy young plantlet.

Starting with seeds

Mail-order catalogs and websites offer a much greater choice of seeds than garden centers. Any reputable supplier will recommend suitable varieties for your local conditions (pp80–81); check also that the variety's growth habit is suitable for you. The cost of seeds may vary, so check the approximate seed count on the packet as well as the price. Seeds of an F1 hybrid are more expensive than open-pollinated seed.

It can be satisfying to buy seeds from small family suppliers, but you should be aware that if they grow a lot of varieties in a small area, there is a greater chance of cross-pollination and therefore variation in the plants. If you are interested in heirloom varieties, it is worth joining one of the non-profit organizations dedicated to the preservation of heirloom seeds. (See p187 for useful websites and addresses.)

CHOOSE YOUR SEEDS – each one is a potential plant

Naked seeds Most seeds are supplied as dried seeds; store in a cool, dry place out of the light and they will keep for a long time.

Pelleted seeds A clay coating makes these seeds easy to handle. Germination rates are less erratic, but they don't keep as long.

Starting with plantlets

Although it is less expensive to raise your own plants from seeds, buying in seedling plants, or plantlets, will save you time that you would otherwise spend raising them yourself. Select good, sturdy plants with deep green leaves that are free from spots and bugs. A good nursery staff should not be upset if they see you checking the undersides of the leaves for insects or lifting a sample plant from its pot to check for vigorous, healthy roots.

If plantlets are particularly small and have undeveloped roots, pot them into 4in (10cm) pots and grow until the roots fill the new pots. When conditions allow, plant any that have flowers (pp98–101).

Tomato plantlets
Buy plantlets in individual cell packs or biodegradable pots, so you can pot or plant them out without any root disturbance.

How to sow seeds

Sowing tomatoes is not a precise science, but for gardeners in temperate regions, it's best to start them 6–8 weeks before the usual date of the last frosts, to give them a long growing season.

Sowing seed too early can result in lanky seedlings, if there is insufficient light early in the season. How much seed you sow depends on how many plants you need. If you need just a few plants, sow up to three seeds in a 3–4in (7.5–10cm) pot. For larger quantities, sow seeds in individual cell packs or seed trays. It is best to use a specifically designed soil mix, because a final potting mix may have too high a level of nutrients, which can actually inhibit germination. Seeds usually germinate after about five days at 64–73°F (18–24°C), but some older varieties may take 2–3 weeks. Make sure that the soil mix does not dry out during this time by covering the container with a plastic bag or placing it in a heated propagator with a lid.

SOWING TOMATO SEEDS INDOORS – sow early for a longer season

1 **Fill a clean container** with soil mix so that it is slightly overfull. Level the surface by drawing a piece of wood across the rim.

2 **Lightly firm the mix** with a block of wood or the back of your hand to create an even sowing surface.

3 Water well with a fine-rosed watering can; alternatively, stand the container in a tray of water until the surface is moist. Drain.

4 Sow the seeds evenly over the surface. It is easier to space the seeds if you trickle them from the palm of your hand.

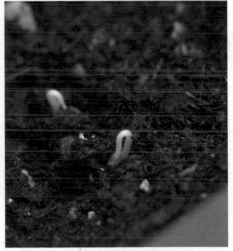

5 Cover the seeds with a thin layer of soil mix, firm, and label. Position in a warm place, such as a windowsill or heated propagator.

6 Once germination begins, remove cover, if used, to decrease humidity and grow the seedlings at 61–68°F (16–20°C).

The first few weeks ...

Watch your seedlings as they begin to grow and the first few leaves appear. Seedlings will be competing for the same water, nutrients, and space to grow, so they will need to be separated into other containers.

The first two leaves to appear are simple, oblong-shaped seed leaves. Once the seedlings have their first pair of true leaves (p12), they can be thinned or pricked out. If you have sown two or three seeds in individual pots or cell packs and you only want one plant, you need to thin them out (below).

Seeds sown thickly in pots or seed trays are at greater risk of fungal infection, so seedlings should be pricked out into individual pots (opposite) as soon as they are large enough to handle. Use clean, 3in (7.5cm) pots filled with moist soil mix.

Grow the pricked-out seedlings indoors in well-ventilated conditions in a bright spot, but not in direct sun, at 61–75°F (16–24°C). They will cope with slightly cooler temperatures overnight. Keep the soil moist, not soggy. There is no need to feed the seedlings at this stage.

THINNING OUT SEEDLINGS – weeding out the weakest

Choose the strongest seedling in each pot or cell pack and remove the others. Simply pull them out gently or, to avoid disturbing the roots of the strongest one, nip them out at soil level with clean scissors or fingernails.

PRICKING OUT SEEDLINGS – handle them with care

1 Hold each seedling by its leaves (the fragile stems are easily damaged) and use a dibble or sturdy plant label to ease the seedling's roots gently from the soil.

2 Plant each seedling in a pot of fresh soil mix, filling in carefully so the seedling is at the same level as before, or slightly deeper if the stem is a bit lanky. Firm gently around the stem and water in well.

Alternatively, make a hole in the center of a filled pot with a pencil or your finger, and lower the seedling roots into the hole. Firm.

Toughening up

Young tomato plants may be planted outside once all danger of frost has passed, but those started off in a protected environment will need a transition period to get them used to the conditions outdoors.

Hardening off is the process of allowing young plants to adapt to the wind, sunlight, and fluctuating temperatures outdoors. Put the plants outdoors for an hour on the first day, two hours on the next, and work up to five or six hours. Avoid exposing them to full sun or wind.

Once plants are hardened off, they can be planted outdoors in suitably prepared soil. Be ready to protect young plants with a layer of horticultural fleece or newspapers in the event of an unexpected cold front.

Hardiness, or ability to withstand cold, is a complex quality in plants. No tomato plants are able to withstand frost, but their ability to cope with cool conditions varies. Some plants such as 'Sub-Arctic Plenty' (p34) can set fruit under quite cool conditions, but others will need shelter to create a favorable microclimate.

Half-way house

You can use a cold frame or cloche as a half-way haven for hardening off young tomato plants, between indoors and out.

In areas with a short growing season, you can also use cold frames and cloches to protect young tomatoes after planting and help extend the season. Make your own (below) or use ready-made models. Another way to shelter a young plant and enable you to plant it out a month or so earlier is a wall o'water—a circle of water-filled plastic bottles around the plant. The water absorbs heat during the day and releases it at night.

Tunnel cloche To make a cloche, drape a horticultural fleece over wire hoops. It will protect plants in the period after planting.

Cold frame Insulate your plants so they slowly acclimatize to cool temperatures. Open the frame at intervals for good ventilation.

Planting

Plant tomato plants into soil beds or containers when they are 6–12in (15–30cm) tall, with well-developed, healthy rootballs. Moist (not soggy) rootballs slip out of pots more easily.

Soil beds

When planting in outdoor beds, use an appropriate support system—try wire cages for bushes and wooden stakes for cordons. Dwarf plants don't need a support. Choose an overcast, still day to reduce stress to the plant from sun and wind and plant in a sheltered spot, such as against a sunny wall or downwind of a hedge or trellis.

PLANT IN A SOIL BED – plant deeply for healthy roots

1 While soaking the plant pot in water or a diluted seaweed solution (for 2–3 hours), dig a planting hole, about twice the pot's depth.

2 Hammer in a sturdy stake next to the planting hole. Remove the plant from its pot and place it into the soil.

3 Backfill with soil so that the stem is covered at least up to the level of the seed leaves. This will encourage new roots to form, which stabilizes the plant and can increase yield, as there are more feeding roots. Firm.

4 Water in well and label. In areas where cutworms are a problem and may nibble the stem, make a tinfoil or cardboard collar and slip it around the base of the stem. This should protect the young plant until it is robust enough to resist attack.

Containers

When you are transferring young tomato plants into containers such as pots, hanging baskets, or growing bags, you need to observe the same basic principles as for planting (pp98–99).

One advantage of containers is that you can start the tomatoes earlier and keep the planted containers under cover until conditions are favorable outdoors, which will give you an earlier crop. You can't do this with growing bags, however, as they are difficult to move once planted.

You may wish to plant a trailing or dwarf tomato plant into a hanging basket. Keep it in a light, airy room, or in the greenhouse, at a minimum of 59°F (15°C), until all risk of frost is past.

Tomato plants in pots and growing bags need a sturdy support system of canes and twine, stakes, or wires on fencing or walls. Bamboo canes are often used, but they may not be able to cope with the weight of some of the more vigorous plants. Opt for stakes in this instance. You can help to hold canes upright in growing bags by tying the top of each cane to a greenhouse strut or some other strong support outdoors such as a trellis.

PLANTING INTO A GROWING BAG – position the bag before planting it

1 Cut 3 planting holes in the plastic. Add a watering funnel (made from a baseless plastic bottle) to avoid water run-off.

2 To plant the bag, water each plant well and insert it in its hole at the same depth or slightly deeper than before. Firm.

Protecting your plants

When positioning containers, choose a spot that provides shelter from strong winds and excessive rain. The most effective barriers are not solid screens such as walls or fences, but those that are around 60 percent permeable, which filter the wind rather than causing damaging eddies. However, in cool areas, tomatoes trained against a sunny wall will benefit from reflected heat.

You can also improve drainage on heavy soils by building raised beds or adding plenty of organic matter to increase the moisture retention of light soils.

Create an effective screen from drying winds by growing climbing plants such as runner beans up a simple trellis screen. >

3 **Punch some drainage holes** into the base of the bag to keep the soil from becoming stagnant, then water the plants thoroughly.

4 **As the plants grow,** tie the main stems to the supports, using soft twine in a figure-eight pattern—don't tie the stems too tightly.

Crop rotation

If you grow tomatoes as part of a larger vegetable plot, you might want to include them in a crop rotation plan, along with the other vegetable crops, to protect them from pests and diseases.

The basics

Growing the same crops year after year in the same soil can lead to a build-up of soil-borne pests and diseases. If you rotate annual crops around the garden so that they are not grown in the same area again for at least three years, you should avoid such a build-up. Closely related vegetables (from the same plant family) are usually grouped together for crop rotation since they will be prone to the same pests and diseases.

The practice of crop rotation has other benefits. It helps to make efficient use of the soil nutrients. Also, alternating between deep-rooted crops and more fibrous-rooted ones can help to improve the soil structure. However, the rotation needs to be carried out over a much longer time frame than the usual three or four years to be completely effective, and keeping to a strict rotation in a small garden may be impractical.

Keep on moving

To follow a four-year crop rotation, divide the vegetable garden into four areas. On the first plot, grow tomatoes and other members of the same (*Solanaceae*) family, such as eggplant and potatoes. You can also include root crops, such as carrots and beets, with this group. In the second year, move the tomatoes and roots to the second plot,

and in the first plot grow members of the onion family. In the third year, move the tomatoes and roots to the third plot, the onions to the second plot, and grow legumes (peas and beans) in the first plot. Most vegetables in the legume family have nodules on their roots; these house bacteria that can fix, or store, nitrogen from the soil, making it available for the following crop.

It is traditional to follow legumes with nitrogen-hungry brassicas, such as cabbages and broccoli, before using the same ground for tomatoes and root crops again. If possible, grow tomatoes and potatoes with a buffer zone of plants between them.

Fallow seasons

Keeping soil fallow—growing nothing on it for a season—will reduce populations of some soil-borne pests, such as root-knot nematodes (microscopic worms); they will die out through lack of food. Dig over the soil to expose the nematodes and other pests to the drying sun and to feeding birds. This will refresh the soil ready for growing next year.

A four-year cycle The photographs opposite show 4 plots of land. Follow the plots to find out what you should grow in each for every year in a 4-year crop rotation. >

Plot One
Year 1 Tomato family Year 2 Onion family
Year 3 Legume family Year 4 Brassica family

Plot Two
Year 1 Brassica family Year 2 Tomato family
Year 3 Onion family Year 4 Legume family

Plot Three
Year 1 Legume family Year 2 Brassica family
Year 3 Tomato family Year 4 Onion family

Plot Four
Year 1 Onion family Year 2 Legume family
Year 3 Brassica family Year 4 Tomato family

A little help from friends

The practice of growing plants that may have a beneficial effect on their neighbors is called companion planting. Plants that repel pests or that attract pollinating insects make good companions for crops.

Keep companion plants 12–24in (30–60cm) from the main stems of tomato plants—close enough to be beneficial, without competing with the tomatoes for nutrients. In a greenhouse or polytunnel, place pots of companions among the crop.

Good companions

Ideal plants to grow with tomatoes include basil, chives, onions, carrots, mint, and parsley. Marigolds, especially the French marigold (*Tagetes patula*), are thought to be particularly good at repelling whitefly (pp116–117) and even nematode pests that may be present in the soil. Marigolds are long-flowering plants and, like nasturtiums (*Tropaeolum majus*), will attract many pollinators. The beautiful, blue-flowered herb, borage (*Borago officinalis*), is said to deter moths that may damage tomato plants (pp116–117).

In greenhouses prone to infestations of whitefly or fungus gnats, it is worth growing a few plants of the common unicorn plant (*Proboscidea louisianica*), also known as the common devil's claw or elephant's tusk. This pretty plant with showy gloxinia-like flowers has oval, wavy-edged leaves that are covered in glandular hairs that sparkle in the light. The leaves are extremely sticky and act as flypaper, catching many small insects. The plant is considered a noxious weed in some US states because the strange, clawed seedpods can damage the eyes of livestock. Allow it only to set sufficient seed to grow a few new plants for the next year.

Friendly fungi

Mycorrhizae are soil-borne fungi that form symbiotic (mutually beneficial) relationships with plants. They colonize the roots of a nearby plant, such as a tomato, and extend their network (mycelium) of fine, sticky filaments, known as hyphae, into the nearby soil. A mycelium increases the surface area of the roots of a host plant, enabling the host to absorb more food and water.

It is also thought that the sticky hyphae protect the plant from soil-borne fungal diseases, making it difficult for them to invade the host.

Mycorrhizae thrive in rich, organic soils, but are destroyed by digging and the high salt content of chemical fertilizers, so organic cultivation methods are thought to be particularly beneficial.

Best friends (clockwise from top left) mint (*Mentha*), chives (*Allium schoenoprasum*), French marigolds, and nasturtium. **>**

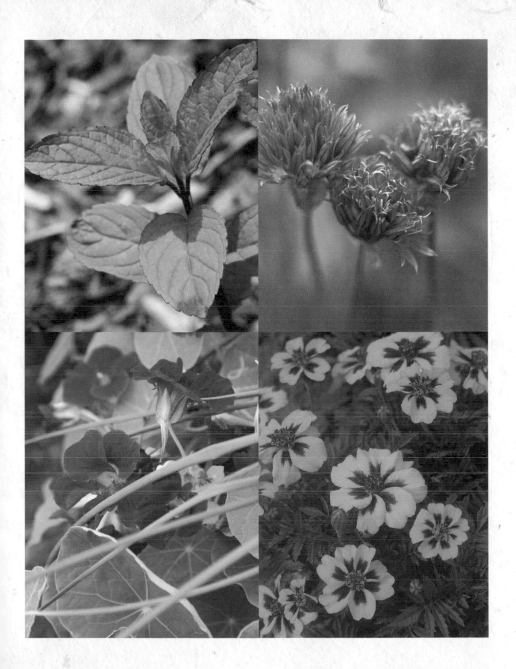

Mulching

Mulch is a protective covering of the soil's surface. It's a good idea to apply mulch just after you have planted to warm the soil and minimize weed growth. Choose from inorganic and organic mulches.

Mulches reduce water loss from the soil, insulate it from excessive cold and heat, and deter weeds. Inorganic mulches, such as black plastic sheets, gravel, or woven membranes, control weeds most effectively. Black mulches absorb heat and warm spring soils, but may overheat soils in hot temperatures. Red plastic mulches reflect intense red light to young plants and may increase crops. Most mulches are applied at planting, but light-colored straw reflects the sun away from the soil, so is better applied once plants are growing strongly. Other organic mulches include dried glass clippings, well-rotted animal manure or bark, wilted comfrey leaves, straw, or layers of newspaper. Mulches should not contain any residual weedkiller, which could harm the tomato plant and crop.

USING INORGANIC MULCH – stop the weeds with a plastic sheet!

1 Lay a weed-suppressing membrane over the soil, then cut flaps in it and pound in a stake. Replace the flaps after planting.

2 Tie the plant to the stake with string and flatten the membrane firmly around the base of the plant.

USING ORGANIC MULCH – these attractive mulches allow water to permeate

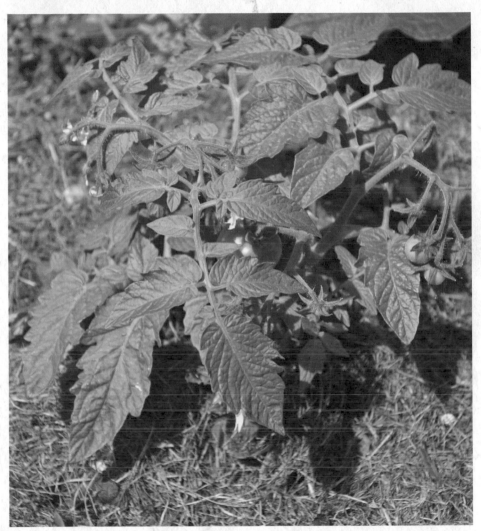

Spread loose organic mulches, such as layers of grass clippings, to a depth of 3in (7.5cm). You can also add more later on as the plant grows. This will stop the soil from drying out and stressing the plant roots.

Food and drink

Like people, plants cannot exist without water, so make sure your tomato plants have enough to drink. Food is important too, and can boost your tomato crop. But with both food and drink, balance is key.

The water of life

Plants need water for transpiration, where moisture evaporates from open pores on their leaves, drawing more water up from their roots through tiny vessels. This process cools the plant and creates a transport system carrying water and nutrients around the plant. Transpiration is greatest in a dry, warm atmosphere and substantially increases in windy conditions. In reasonably sunny conditions, a typical tomato plant needs about ¾ quart (1½ pints) of water per day. This varies greatly, depending on the type and state of the soil or mix and how well it drains, the stage of growth of the plant, and the weather. Container-grown plants need plenty of water because their roots cannot spread far. Feel the soil below the surface with your finger to see if it needs water.

Water with care Roots need a moist, but not wet, growing medium. Soggy soils can be low in oxygen levels, leading to root death.

Split skin Irregular watering may lead to fruit splitting (pp118–119). Excessive watering may also produce large but tasteless fruits.

To feed or not to feed

Plants grown in open, well-nourished soil usually yield a good tomato crop without additional feeding. For the best crop from plants in pots or growing bags, feed them regularly after the first truss of fruit has set. Nitrogen (N), phosphorus (P), potassium (K), and calcium (Ca) are the most important minerals in tomato fertilizer.

Most homemade plant feed has a bad smell, but are a cheap way of feeding your plants organically. Fill a container with comfrey leaves, nettles, or other fresh green weeds and pour boiling water over them. Cover and steep for a month, then strain the liquid and use well diluted in water. You could also use the liquid by-product from a wormery.

Too much fertilizer can be harmful to plants, so always follow the manufacturer's recommended dosages. Overfed plants may make excessive, soft growth, which will be vulnerable to disease and may delay flowering. A build-up of chemical salts in soil can also damage root growth. Never use lawn fertilizer on tomatoes: this is high in nitrogen, which will encourage lots of leafy growth rather than fruits.

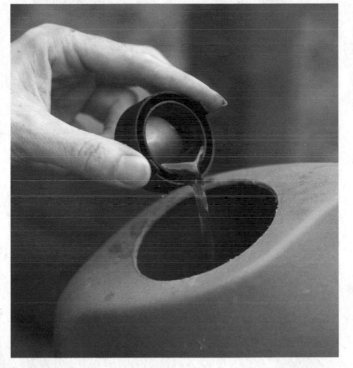

Using a fertilizer
Specifically formulated fertilizer for tomatoes will ensure that your plants receive the right balance of nutrients.

Removing sideshoots

Making sure you prune sideshoots from your tomato plant regularly will ensure that it stays healthy. Keep your cuttings and use them to make new plants to increase your own crop or give them to friends.

Removing sideshoots produces a single stem, or cordon, which makes your plants easier to support and admits more air and water to their fruits. There is no need to remove sideshoots from bush or trailing types. The sideshoots form in every leaf axil—pinch them off regularly as soon as they can be handled. Cut off larger sideshoots at their bases to avoid tearing the main stem. In very hot climates, allow each sideshoot to produce one leaf. This will protect the fruits from potential sun damage. When the cordon reaches the top of its support, pinch off the growing tips to encourage the fruits to ripen; also pinch off any flowers toward the end of the season. To create new plants, take side shoots early in the season, so that the new plants have long enough to ripen their fruits.

CUTTINGS ARE EASY! – recycle sideshoots into new plants

1 **Choose a sideshoot** that is reasonably firm at its base and can be handled easily, and snap it cleanly from the main stem.

2 **Place the sideshoot** in a jar or glass of clean water. Brown glass aids speedy rooting, but roots should appear anyway within a week.

3 **Pot the sideshoot** carefully, once its roots are at least ½–¾in (1–2cm) long, in a pot of seed mix.

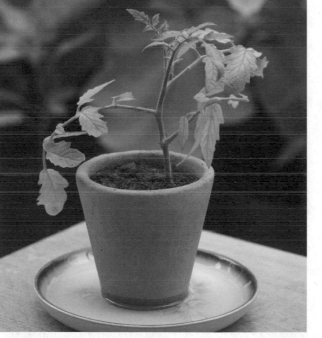

4 **Firm gently** to avoid damaging the fragile roots, and water in. Grow the cutting in the same way as a new seedling (pp94–95).

Large sideshoots of 12in (30cm) or more will root successfully, but keep them shaded or they may wilt.

Pollination

For a tomato plant to form a fruit, the stigma, or female part of a flower, must be fertilized by viable pollen. This will occur naturally with assistance from insects and wind, but you can help too ...

Cultivated tomato plants are self-fertile—they can fertilize flowers with their own pollen. When the flower opens, pollen falls from the anthers, or male parts of the flower, onto the stigma. If the atmosphere is too dry, pollen will not stick to the stigma; in very wet conditions, pollen is not released from the anthers.

The optimal temperature for pollination is 65–80°F (18.5–26.5°C). In very cold conditions, very little fruit will set, whereas very hot conditions kill the pollen. Since there are fewer insects to pollinate flowers under cover, you can help yourself. Wait until there are many trusses of ripe flowers and carry it out at noon, when pollen is most abundant.

POLLINATING TOMATO FLOWERS – play Cupid to guarantee a good crop

1 The female part of the tomato flower (stigma) lies in most plants within a cone of pollen-bearing (male) anthers (bottom left).

2 Gently shake the flower clusters. Tapping the plant's wire or cane supports will also encourage the pollen to be released.

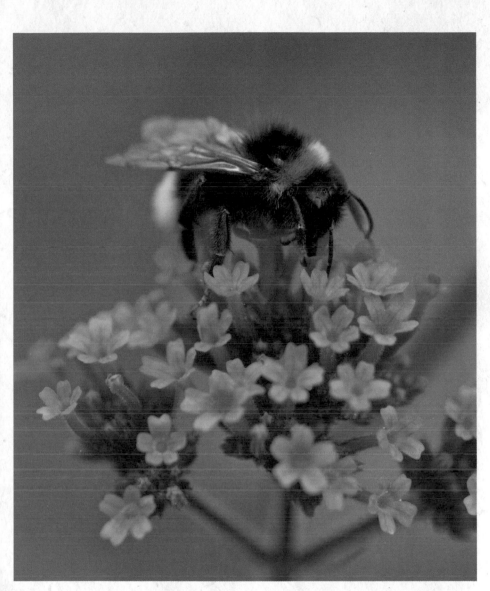

Busy bees Insects, such as the bumblebee (*Bombus terrestris*), play a vital role in pollination. As they collect nectar, they fly from plant to plant and distribute pollen. Many commercial units utilize this by installing colonies of bumblebees in cardboard hives among the tomato crops.

Pests and diseases

Healthy plants are better able to cope with pests and diseases and produce good crops, so it is important to identify and control any problems. The first step is to use good cultivation techniques.

Choose disease-resistant plants

Most modern F1 hybrid tomato plants are relatively disease resistant, as commercial plant breeders work to improve resistance to a number of fungal and other pathogens. Verticillium and fusarium wilts, for example, are soil-borne diseases that cause yellowing of the leaves, wilting, and premature death of plants. Once they build up in the soil, the only practical control is the use of resistant varieties, such as 'Roma' (p65), which are often designated by the letters "VF" in seed catalogs. "VFN" indicates a variety, such as 'Lemon Boy' (p35), that is also resistant to root-knot nematodes, wormlike pests that live in the soil. There are few blight-tolerant plants, although 'Ferline' (p23) and 'Legend' (p55) are particularly disease resistant.

Prevention is better than cure

Compacted, poorly drained soil stresses the plants, so prepare the soil well (pp88–89). Practice crop rotation (pp102–103) to avoid growing tomatoes after crops in the same family, which are prone to the same diseases. Eradicate weeds, particularly those in the nightshade family, which may harbor disease organisms. Maintain good plant hygiene by removing and destroying all infected plant material—do not put infected material on a compost heap because some pests and diseases may survive and infect subsequent crops. Space plants to encourage air circulation and reduce spread of pests or diseases. Staking and removing sideshoots (pp110–111) promote air flow around plants. Try to keep the foliage dry to minimize fungal infections. Position plants where they benefit from the morning sun to dry out any dew from the leaves. Avoid watering the plants from overhead, particularly if it is late in the day.

A note about late blight

Late blight is the most common and most deadly problem that may affect your crop. It can have a devastating affect particularly in cool, wet climates. Do not leave unharvested potatoes in the soil, as they can be a source of infection to subsequent crops. If buying transplants, check carefully to ensure you buy healthy stock. Growing tomato plants under cover will provide some protection from wind-blown spores. Use the charts on the following pages if your plant is showing signs of ill health.

Common problems with tomato plants include (clockwise from top left): early blight, late blight, blossom end rot, and sapfeeding whitefly. >

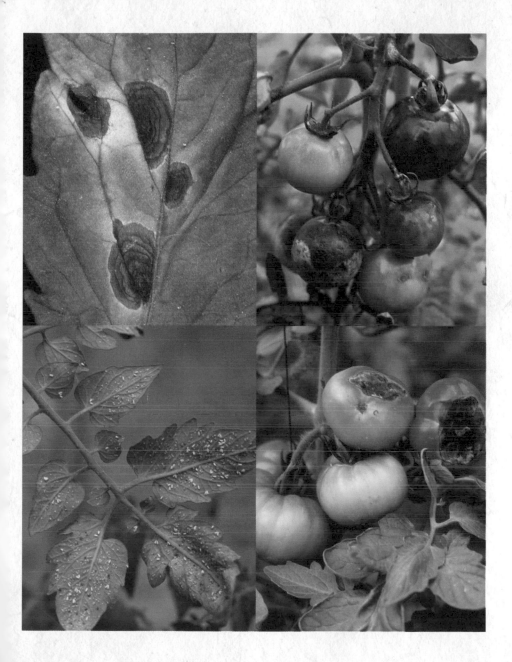

What's wrong with my leaves?

You can often distinguish a healthy plant from an unhealthy plant by its leaves, as they are usually the first to show symptoms of pests and diseases. Sometimes, however, changes in leaf appearance may be a result of changes in temperature, and are no cause for concern.

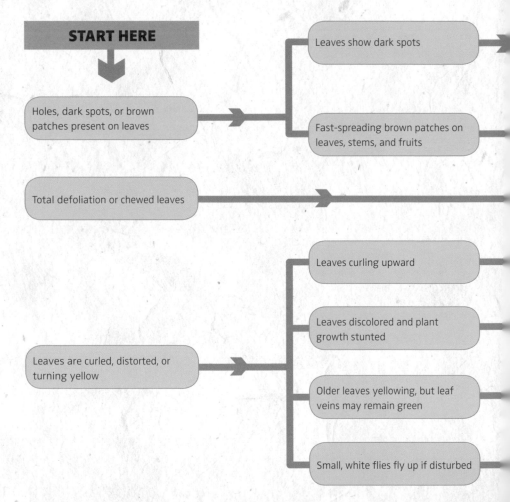

START HERE

Holes, dark spots, or brown patches present on leaves

Leaves show dark spots

Fast-spreading brown patches on leaves, stems, and fruits

Total defoliation or chewed leaves

Leaves curling upward

Leaves discolored and plant growth stunted

Leaves are curled, distorted, or turning yellow

Older leaves yellowing, but leaf veins may remain green

Small, white flies fly up if disturbed

CAUSE and TREATMENT

Spots often have concentric rings with a faded yellowing around them, particularly on lower leaves

→ **Early blight** (*Alternaria* species) is a fungal infection – Remove and destroy all affected leaves immediately

Spots often have a thin circle of bright yellow surrounding them

→ **Bacterial leaf spot** – Remove all affected leaves and avoid wetting other foliage during watering

Late blight (*Phytophthora infestans*) – Destroy affected plants; use copper-based fungicide as preventative spray

Tomato hornworm (of five-spotted hawkmoth) – Pick off pests or use biological control (*Bacillus thuringiensis*)

May be sign of **leaf roll virus**, but usually a result of cold nights – Will not affect the plant's growth

Viruses such as **tomato mosaic virus** or **curly top virus** – Destroy affected plants and control aphids

Magnesium deficiency – Apply magnesium sulphate (Epsom salts) as a dilute solution to plant leaves

Sapfeeding whitefly (*Trialeurodes vaporariorum*) – Use sticky traps or biological control (*Encarsia formosa*)

What's wrong with my tomatoes?

Keep an eye on developing fruits so that you can take action as soon as any symptoms of pests or diseases appear to avoid more fruits being affected. Some problems with your tomatoes can be resolved by simply watering them more regularly.

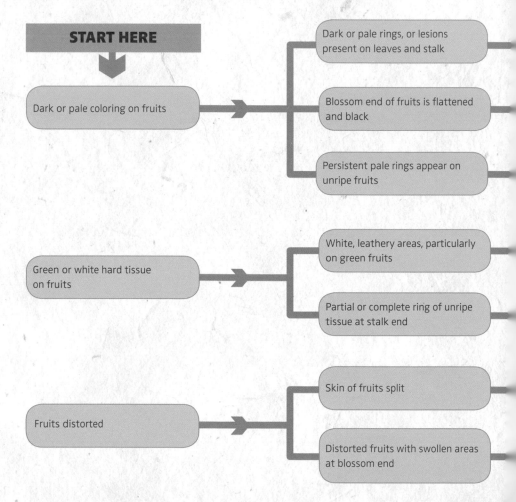

START HERE

Dark or pale coloring on fruits

- Dark or pale rings, or lesions present on leaves and stalk
- Blossom end of fruits is flattened and black
- Persistent pale rings appear on unripe fruits

Green or white hard tissue on fruits

- White, leathery areas, particularly on green fruits
- Partial or complete ring of unripe tissue at stalk end

Fruits distorted

- Skin of fruits split
- Distorted fruits with swollen areas at blossom end

Dark, concentric rings on stalk ends of fruits

Early blight (*Alternaria* species) is a fungal infection – Remove and destroy all affected leaves immediately

Lesions on fruits are olive-brown colored

Late blight (*Phytophthora infestans*) – Destroy affected plants; use copper-based fungicide as preventative spray

Blossom end rot – lack of calcium caused by irregular watering; Control watering; apply feed of soluble calcium

Ghost spots caused by fungus (*Botrytis cinerea*) – Improve air circulation

Sunscald – Provide shading for plants

Greenback – usually caused by heat injury; Apply shading or choose resistant plants

Fruit splitting – caused by irregular watering and extremes of temperature; Water regularly

Catfacing – caused by poor pollination; Apply shade and damp down green-house if hot, put in sunny area if cold

what's wrong with my tomatoes? **119**

Reaping the harvest

For the home gardener, the reward of a succulent, sun-ripened tomato that is rich in flavor is the ultimate goal, and so the fruits should be left on the plant to ripen to the peak of perfection.

The ripe stuff

The process of tomato ripening is governed by the temperature—a range of 65–75°F (18–24°C) is best for most varieties. As ripening gets under way, the green pigment (chlorophyll) breaks down and the orange-yellow (beta-carotene) and red (lycopene) pigments increase. It is the relative concentrations of the latter pigments that determine the color of a ripe tomato.

Take your pick

Pick fruits as soon as they ripen so that the plant keeps producing new tomatoes. This is particularly important toward the end of the season, when you want the plant to concentrate on swelling the remaining fruits.

You can also help along the ripening process later in the season by removing any yellowing leaves from the bases of plants, to let in more sunlight to the tomatoes.

PICKING TOMATOES – find the ripest, juiciest tomatoes, pick, and enjoy

Small fruits Rather than picking lots of small fruits, it is easier to cut off the entire truss, with pruning shears or a sharp garden knife.

Large fruits Apply slight pressure with your thumb where stem and calyx join (abscission layer, or knuckle). Gently twist and break off.

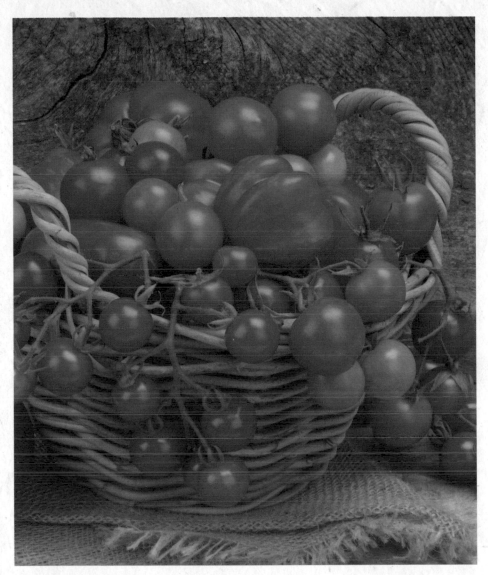

Kitchen marvels The reward of spending just a few hours a week in your garden. Turn to page 132 to see how to enjoy them.

Beat the autumn frosts

Try to harvest all tomato fruits before the first frost. They may continue to ripen indoors (below), if picked immediately after a light frost, but a heavy frost will damage the internal tissues; use any frost-damaged tomatoes right away.

While the first frosts are light, you may untie a cordon plant from its support, lay it flat on the ground, and cover it with a layer of horticultural fleece. The tomatoes may then continue to ripen on the plants while being protected from a few degrees of frost. Take in the fruits if heavy frost is forecasted.

The last of the crop

At the end of the season, hang trusses of tomatoes to ripen (opposite). There is a group of tomatoes known as long-keeper varieties, such as the Spanish 'De Colgar,' which ripen slowly after harvesting if kept in a cool, frost-free place. They can take up to three months to reach maturity and should be ready for eating in winter, long after you have eaten your main-crop tomatoes.

There are occasional reports of tomatoes that remain in good condition for up to a year, but the mechanisms of fruit longevity are not fully understood at present.

RIPENING INDIVIDUAL TOMATOES – all you need is patience

Go bananas – put green tomatoes in a bowl next to a banana: it emits ethylene gas, which encourages the tomatoes to ripen.

RIPENING TRUSSES – so tempting, they may be eaten off the line!

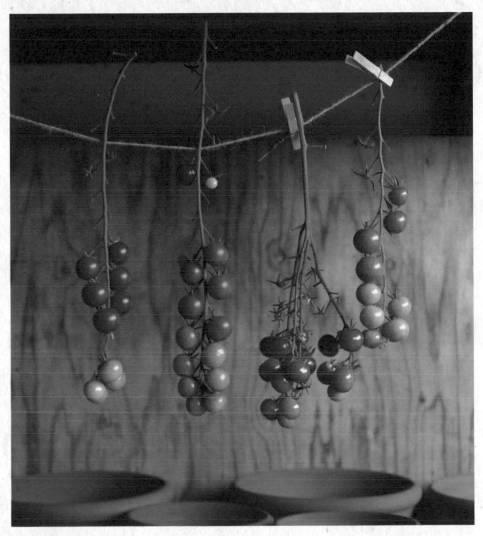

Cut trusses of green tomatoes and hang in
an airy place such as a garage, potting shed,
spare bedroom, or even the kitchen, to ripen.

Save your favorite seeds

If you have a favorite tomato that grows well in your garden, it is well worth saving the seeds for next year. Most tomatoes are self-pollinating, so the offspring will be identical to the parent plant.

However, if you or any of your neighbors grow several tomato plants within a bee's flight path, there is a risk that the plants will cross-pollinate. If so, the seedlings may vary from the parent. Currant tomatoes and many large beefsteak varieties have stigmas that protrude beyond the anthers, so are particularly vulnerable to cross-pollination. This may not worry you, but if you plan to donate seeds to a seed exchange, isolate the parent plant or bag individual trusses with a light muslin bag or cheesecloth, secured below the truss with a rubber band around the stem.

Tomato seeds are coated with a gel that protects them from attack by seed-borne diseases, like bacterial spot and early blight (pp114–119), but also inhibits germination. When preparing seeds for storage, you can remove the gel by fermentation.

STORING SEEDS – a cool, dark place keeps seeds viable for longer

Keep your seeds in labeled envelopes or paper sachets (plastic bags encourage mold) in an airtight container with a sachet of silica gel to absorb moisture. Store in a cool, dark place, preferably in the salad drawer of the refrigerator.

DRYING – a simple method for a small amount of seeds

1 **Collect seeds** from ripe or even over-ripe fruits. Slice each tomato in half; scrape out the seeds with the point of a sharp knife.

2 **To save only a few** seeds, simply leave them to dry on a paper towel, but spread them out well so they do not get moldy.

FERMENTING – good for large quantities of seeds

1 **Scoop the pulpy seeds** into a jar and leave in a warm place. After two days, a yeasty smell will indicate that the gel is fermenting.

2 **Once the seeds** are gel-free (a white fungal layer should form after 5–7 days), rinse the seeds. Spread out for a week to dry.

All for show

The record for the largest tomato was set in 1986 by Gordon Graham of Oklahoma, for a 'Delicious' weighing 7lb 12oz (3.51kg). Record-breaking or just for fun, showing tomatoes can be very satisfying.

Which class?

Usually, shows run by national organizations have traditional classes, but a local show may have a class for the ugliest or heaviest vegetable. Classes for 6–8 fruits require tomatoes of uniform size and color, with intact, fresh, green calyces.

Grooming marvelous

Good soil preparation is important: work in plenty of organic matter to feed the plant. A sunny site is best for growth, but protect fruits from sunscald in very hot weather. Water regularly and apply a high-potash, or potassium (K), feed. Thin show tomatoes to five fruits per truss for the best shape and size. Support very large tomatoes; old nylons are stretchy and do not cut into the fruits. Protect ripening tomatoes from birds with netting or horticultural fleece.

It's all in the timing

Timing is vital in growing for exhibition. It is no good producing a perfect crop of evenly matched fruit if they do not ripen in the week of the show. Many variables affect maturation, chiefly sunlight and prevailing temperatures. The average number of days to maturity is often listed on seed packets, but these may vary greatly. The figure may be given as days from germination to first picking or as days from planting.

Exhibition growers often sow three or more batches of seeds at two-weekly intervals to ensure ripe tomatoes on the required day. Do not start your plants too early; even with grow-lights, it can be difficult to keep plants growing strongly. If you want giant fruits, expect it to take 140–150 days from sowing seed to harvesting a ripe tomato.

A couple of days before the show, collect twice as many fruits as you need and place in a dark place to finish ripening. Select the best fruits on the day of the show. If fruit ripens too early, hold them back in the refrigerator at around 50°F (10°C) for up to three weeks; never freeze them, as they turn to mush on thawing. On the day of the show, label and present with care.

Varieties to show off

Good classic, round, F1 tomatoes include 'Cedrico,' 'Cleopatra,' and 'Vandos.' For giant fruits, try 'Slankards,' 'Omar's Lebanese,' or the hybrid 'Big Zac.'

Perfection Show fruits must be just ripe. >

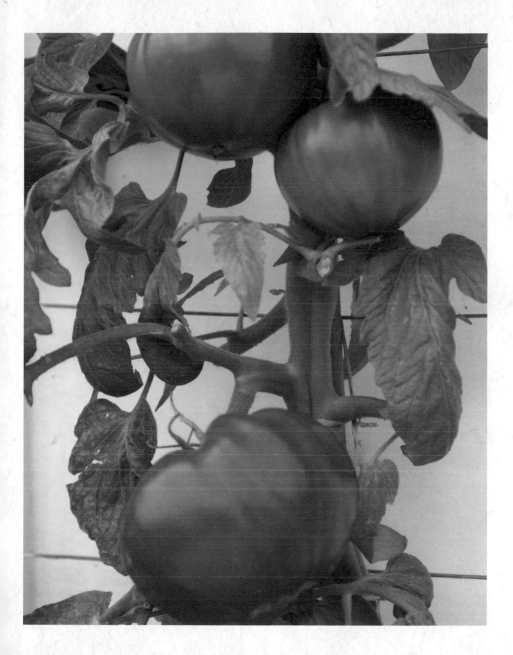

Get grafting

Grafting is a way of joining two plants together so that they benefit from each other's strengths. It is fairly simple to carry out and is ideal if a particular tomato plant does not usually grow well for you.

Grafting allows a tomato variety to take on advantageous qualities of another tomato plant, usually a more robust species or variety. By grafting your chosen variety onto a rootstock, it is possible to promote growth, increase fruit quality and yield, and confer other benefits such as tolerance of low temperatures and resistance to soil-borne diseases. You may buy seeds of tomato rootstocks, such as 'KNVF,' 'Beaufort,' and 'Brigeor.' Alternatively, use any tomato plant that you have found to be particularly resilient in your garden.

A graft should unite after 7–10 days: remove the cover and plant or pot the plant. Rub off any shoots emerging below the graft point (they will be more vigorous and overwhelm the grafted plant).

HOW TO GRAFT – combining the best qualities of two plants

1 **Take the rootstock plant**, and with pruning shears or a clean, sharp knife, cut straight across to leave a short stem.

2 **Make a vertical cut** downward about ½in (2cm) with a sharp knife into the center of the rootstock stem.

3 Cut a healthy shoot from your chosen tomato plant. It should have a stem of a similar width to the rootstock.

4 Make two sloping cuts at the base of the stem, on opposite sides and about ½in (2cm) long, to create a tapered end.

5 Insert the tapered end of the shoot into the cut on the rootstock. Bind the graft with soft surgical or grafting tape or a grafting clip.

6 Cover with a plastic bottle or bag to keep humid and place in a cool, shaded position until the graft heals. Water regularly.

Create a variety of your very own

It is always fun to try to produce something new—so why not breed a hybrid tomato for your own family to treasure? Breeding tomatoes is not difficult and requires only a little patience.

You may identify traits that you would like; for example, you might wish that 'Black Cherry' (p38) was available in a dwarf trailing form such as that of 'Tumbler' (p36). Crossing these two varieties and selecting the best offspring over a few generations may lead to a new plant with the desired characteristics. You may end up with many plants showing the growth habit of 'Black Cherry' and the fruits of 'Tumbler,' but that is part of the fun.

The first step in breeding tomatoes is to cross-pollinate the two chosen parents (below). Collect seeds from the female (seed-bearing) parent and raise new plants from them. Be ready to grow many seedlings and keep crossing their offspring. If you do produce a plant worth keeping, isolate it and save the seeds for 3–5 years to ensure that it is stable. Then you can name it and, if you wish, offer it to commercial seed suppliers.

HOW TO CROSS-POLLINATE A TOMATO – create unique seeds

1 Remove all anthers (pp112–113) from a newly open flower with fingers or tweezers to create a seed-bearing parent.

2 Rub the anthers of the pollen parent over the stigma of the seed-bearing parent. Label with names of both parents.

Your perfect tomato plants Start a family of plants to create your perfect crop. Watch them grow, then have fun naming them.

In the
kitchen

Store your tomatoes at room temperature to keep their wonderful flavor. Then, use the simple techniques at the beginning of this chapter to prepare, cook, and preserve them. The selection of recipes—from Cream of tomato soup to Tomato and Gruyère tart to Ice cream—will make the most of your home-grown crop. Try making a recipe that is perfect for zesty, green fruits or one that is great for a glut. Enjoy!

Preparation

Preparing tomatoes starts with two things: a good wooden cutting board and a set of sharp knives for peeling, coring, slicing, and chopping. For large, meaty tomatoes, a potato peeler can also come in handy.

Paring knife This is ideal for coring and for peeling blanched tomatoes. You can also use it to scoop out any seeds.

Short blade and pointed tip

Small serrated knife You will use this time and time again. It cuts through tomato skins very easily without becoming dull.

Serrated blade

Chef's knife With its very sharp blade, this is great for slicing and chopping peeled tomatoes, as well for dicing.

Broad fine-edged blade

SLICING – for all types of tomatoes

Place the tomato on your cutting board and, using a serrated knife, cut into slices from the bottom to the top; discard the ends.

LONG-SLICING – for larger tomatoes

Using a chef's knife, cut into quarters and seed (p139). Lie flat and slice thinly on the diagonal.

CHOPPING AND DICING – for all types of medium to large tomatoes

Once you have cut your tomatoes into long slices (above), gather them under your hand and position so that they are perpendicular to the knife. Chop coarsely, or cut into dice as thinly as you need (the latter is known as a concassée.)

PEELING – for tomatoes to be eaten in salads

Using a serrated knife, make a small incision near the stem end. Peel carefully, rotating the tomato as you go, as though you were peeling an apple.

SKINNING BY CHARRING – very good for plum, globe, and cherry varieties

1 **Using tongs or a fork**, hold the tomato over an open flame until the skin is blistered. For a smoky taste, char on a charcoal grill.

2 **When the tomato is black all over**, put in a plastic bag to sweat. Cool slightly, then use a blunt knife to peel away the skin.

SKINNING BY BLANCHING – ideal for plum and globe varieties

1 Cut a small cross on the bottom of each tomato. Blanch in very hot water for 15–20 seconds until the skins start to loosen.

2 Have a bowl of ice-cold water ready. Plunge the tomatoes into this to refresh. Remove with a slotted spoon.

3 Once the tomatoes are cool enough to handle, use a knife to peel away the skin.

CORING – useful for large, chunky tomatoes, which can have "woody" cores

Use a paring knife to remove the core from tomatoes while they are still whole. Simply make a conical incision in the top of the tomato, slicing around in a circle; pull out the core and discard.

SEEDING – don't throw the seeds away—save them for making dressings

1 Use a **paring knife** to cut the tomatoes into quarters. Lie them flat on a cutting board and slice off the central core. The seeds and jellylike juices will now easily slide out.

2 **Using a teaspoon** or your fingers, scoop out the seeds and jellylike juice. If you do this over a bowl or jar, you can reserve the juice for other uses, such as to add extra flavoring to a variety of dishes and to make dressings (p177). To remove the seeds, press through a fine sieve.

preparation **139**

Cooking

A side dish of cooked tomatoes—simply fried, roasted, or grilled—makes an excellent accompaniment to many main courses. Use these three simple techniques to cook up a storm with your tomatoes.

The basic methods for cooking tomatoes can be applied and expanded on in so many ways, and tomatoes married with such a diverse combination of ingredients, that you could easily fill shelves and shelves with tomato recipe books. Hopefully, you will find some useful, easy, and delicious recipes to tempt you in the next section, but you can use these basic techniques as building blocks. Experiment with tomato varieties and with other ingredients. Trust your taste buds, and enjoy your time in the kitchen.

GRILLING AND CHAR-GRILLING – under the broiler, in a pan, or on the grill

Char-grilling in a ridged cast-iron grill pan or on a griddle is a great method for plum, globe and even cherry tomatoes. Simply arrange the tomatoes in a very hot pan—there is no need to add oil. Let sizzle, turning from time to time, until they are charred but not burned.

PAN-FRYING – halved, quartered, sliced, or chopped: the choice is yours

Pan-frying works well with globe, plum, and cherry tomatoes. Heat a little olive oil or butter, or a mixture of both, in a pan. Add the tomatoes and sauté, stirring occasionally, until softened. Season and serve. If you like, start by sautéeing some chopped onion first, then add a little garlic, and then add your tomatoes. Sometimes simple is best.

ROASTING – choose your seasonings, drizzle with a little olive oil, and roast

Roasting is great for most tomato varieties. Line a roasting pan with parchment paper. Fill with halved, quartered, or even sliced tomatoes. Add peeled garlic cloves, lemon slices, and some thyme or oregano. Drizzle with a little olive oil, season, and roast in the oven at 350°F (180°C) for 25–30 minutes. For sweetly flavored slow-roasted tomatoes, roast at 275°F (140°C) for at least 2 hours.

Preserving

Keeping otherwise perishable food for long periods of time is a very old technique, known as preserving. It is a great way of ensuring that you can enjoy the fruits of your garden all year round.

Sterilizing jars and bottles

Always use sterilized canning jars with new lids. Wash in very hot, soapy water, then boil the jars and lids in water for 10 minutes. Remove and carefully fill a hot jar to just under ½in (1cm) of the rim. Cover with a lid and immediately affix the screw band according to manufacturer's instructions. When canning whole peeled and cored tomatoes, you need to sterilize them again as they cook. Follow the instructions that come with the jars, or visit www.usda.gov for details. Stand the jars upright in a deep pot with an inverted heatproof plate or a wire rack set on the bottom. Cover with warm water until at least 1in (2.5cm) above the jars. Cover and boil gently for 45–55 minutes. Carefully remove the jars and let sit overnight on a clean dry cloth. Store in a cool, dark place.

DRYING AND REHYDRATING – use any halved and seeded tomatoes

1 To dry, place skin-side down on a wire rack set over a baking sheet. Bake at 150°F (75°C) for 6 hours. Turn over and roast for another 3 hours at 125°F (50°C) or until very dry.

2 To rehydrate, soak dried tomatoes in hot water mixed with olive oil for 5–10 minutes. Barely cover the tomatoes with water; the concentrated liquid can be used later for cooking.

SMOKING – globes and plums

Put dried tomatoes on a wok grill over wood chips. Let smoke, covered, on medium heat in a ventilated room, for about 15 minutes.

MAKING PRESERVES – spice on hand

Always sterilize jars (opposite) for chutney (p150), ketchup (p158), and jam before filling, sealing, and labeling.

CANNING – peeled globes and plums

Pack tomatoes into the sterilized jar and add 2 tbsp of bottled lemon juice; sprinkle with salt as you go. Preserve as given opposite.

FREEZING – suitable for sauce

Tomato sauce such as passata or marinara (p153) can be frozen in zipper-seal plastic bags. Reheat until piping hot before serving.

Tomato borscht

Borscht comes in many variations, depending on its origins. In Russia and the Ukraine, it often includes tomatoes as well as beets. This version may seem a bit unusual at first, but you will fall in love with its rich color and fantastic taste—perfect for an elegant starter.

Serves 4
Prep time: 25 minutes
Cooking time: 25 minutes

2 tbsp olive oil

1 small onion, finely chopped

1 garlic clove, chopped

8oz (225g) raw beets, peeled and finely grated

1 tsp freshly ground toasted cumin seeds (see note)

½ tsp ground cinnamon

8oz (225g) ripe fresh tomatoes, skinned and coarsely chopped

1 cup tomato juice

1 tbsp very finely chopped sun-dried tomatoes

2 cups vegetable stock

1 tbsp soy sauce

sea salt and freshly ground black pepper

To serve

toasted cumin seeds

sour cream or crème fraîche

1 Heat the oil in a heavy pan over low heat. Gently cook the onion and garlic for about 5 minutes, then add the beets. Cook gently for 10 minutes longer, stirring from time to time, until softened but not browned.

2 Add the ground spices, fresh tomatoes, tomato juice, and sun-dried tomatoes, then pour in the stock. Bring to a boil. Reduce the heat slightly, cover, and simmer very gently for 15 minutes or until all the vegetables are soft. Remove from the heat. Blend or process until velvety smooth. Check the seasoning, adding the soy sauce, salt, and pepper to taste.

3 Serve chilled, at room temperature, or slightly warm. If you do reheat the soup, do so gently over low heat. To serve, spoon into soup bowls and garnish with toasted cumin seeds and a spoonful of sour cream or crème fraîche.

Note For the best, most flavorful results, toast whole cumin seeds in a dry frying pan over medium heat for a few minutes until golden and aromatic. Grind to a powder using a mortar and pestle. Use immediately.

Eva's Purple Ball (p31)

Works well with
Standard globe (pp22–35)
Plum (pp64–73)

Cream of tomato soup

In this extra-special version of an old standard, the tomato is the star. Here we have tomatoes in all variations: fresh, sun-dried, and roasted. Inspired by tomato-lovers, this velvety smooth soup takes the humble tomato to a dimension where it rightfully belongs.

Serves 4–6
Prep time: 30 minutes
Cooking time: 40 minutes

3½ tbsp butter

1 tbsp olive oil

2 onions, finely chopped

2 celery ribs, finely chopped

2 carrots, finely chopped

2 garlic cloves, minced

12 plum tomatoes, about 2¼lb (1kg), quartered, roasted (p156), and coarsely chopped, plus 8 extra 1¼–1½lb (600–720g), skinned and finely chopped

6 sun-dried tomatoes, finely chopped

4 cups hot vegetable stock

2–3 tbsp heavy cream

sea salt and freshly ground black pepper

1 Heat the butter and olive oil in a heavy saucepan over medium heat. Add the onions and sauté for 8–10 minutes, stirring frequently, until very soft but not browned. Add the celery and carrots and continue cooking gently for 10 minutes longer. Add the garlic and cook for 2 minutes, stirring occasionally.

2 Mix together the roasted plum tomatoes, sun-dried tomatoes, and fresh tomatoes. Turn into the pan with any juices and cook, stirring, for 5 minutes to blend the flavors. If the sauce looks too thick or starts sticking to the bottom of the pan, add a little of the hot vegetable stock. Pour in the remaining vegetable stock and let the soup simmer for 15–20 minutes.

3 Blend the soup into a smooth purée using a food processor or hand-held blender. Pass through a sieve or food mill placed over a clean pan. Add the cream, 1 teaspoon at a time, until you are happy with the taste and texture. Season with salt and pepper. Reheat very gently, if needed, and serve.

Variation For a peasant-style soup, don't pass the soup through a sieve or food mill. Simply stir in a little cream, and season to taste.

Works well with
Plum (pp64–73)
Beefsteak (pp52–63)
Standard globe (pp22–35)

Salsa romesco

Romesco, Catalan in origin, is a pounded sauce that features two key ingredients: tomatoes and romesco peppers. In Catalunya, festivals are held to celebrate this dish, and families treasure their recipes as closely guarded secrets. Be sure to use the ripest, most flavorful tomatoes.

Makes 1 large bowl
Prep time: 25 minutes
Cooking time: 30 minutes

1 dried nyora (ñora) chile pepper or, for variety, any other hot dried pepper such as cascabel, guajillo, or pimento

20 blanched almonds

2 x 1in (2.5cm) slices of day-old baguette

1 large beefsteak tomato, about 10oz (280g), peeled, quartered, and seeded

3 garlic cloves, unpeeled

¼ cup dry red wine

4 tsp red wine vinegar

½ cup good-quality olive oil

sea salt and freshly ground black pepper

1 Preheat the oven to 350°F (180°C).

2 Seed the dried pepper, and use your hands to tear the flesh into small pieces. Put in a bowl with 3 tablespoons of boiling water, and let stand for about 15 minutes. Drain off the soaking water, reserving the chile.

3 Meanwhile, put the tomato quarters, bread, garlic, and almonds in a roasting pan, sprinkle with a little olive oil, and bake in the oven. Keep an eye on things because the various ingredients take different amounts of time to bake. Allow 5–8 minutes for the almonds, 10 minutes or so for the bread, and about 15 minutes for the tomatoes and garlic.

4 Using a mortar and pestle, pound together the peppers and roasted tomatoes, bread, garlic, and almonds until you have a thick paste. Alternatively, puree in a food processor. Add the red wine and the vinegar, then very gradually add about ½ cup olive oil, pounding or processing as you go, until you have a rich, dark sauce. Season with salt and pepper. Enjoy with grilled meats and seafood, or add to soups and other dishes for an extra kick, or to mayonnaise for added spice.

Note To make your *salsa romesco* even richer, add 2 or 3 coarsely chopped sun-dried tomatoes. If using sun-dried tomatoes packed in olive oil, simply drain first, and pound along with the other ingredients. Sun-dried tomatoes not stored in oil should be soaked with the pepper before using.

Works well with
Beefsteak (pp52–63)
Plum (pp64–73)

Pasta with fresh tomato sauce

An herby "pesto" or "picada" made with sun-dried tomatoes, transforms this sauce into something quite memorable. To enliven the sauce even further, try adding 2 finely chopped anchovies (preferably those preserved in oil) and some very thinly sliced fennel bulb.

Serves 4–6
Prep time: 15–20 minutes
Cooking time: 10 minutes

2 tbsp good-quality extra virgin olive oil

2 roasted garlic cloves (see note)

2 tbsp coarsely chopped flat-leaf parsley

2 tsp chopped fresh oregano or 1 tsp dried

½ tsp *pimentón picante* (Spanish hot smoked paprika)

3 sun-dried tomatoes in olive oil, drained (reserve the oil)

4 large ripe tomatoes, about 1lb (400g), chopped

2 x 14½oz (400g) cans good-quality peeled plum tomatoes, drained and coarsely chopped

generous pinch of light brown sugar

2 tbsp sherry vinegar

1lb (500g) dried pasta such as spaghetti, fusilli, fregula, orecchiette, or tortiglioni

2½ cups fresh arugula leaves

sea salt and freshly ground black pepper

freshly grated or shaved Parmesan cheese, to serve

1 Using a mortar and pestle, pound the olive oil, roasted garlic, parsley, oregano, paprika, and sun-dried tomatoes into a paste that resembles pesto. Alternatively, process briefly in a small blender until a coarse pesto forms. If needed, add a little of the reserved oil from the sun-dried tomatoes.

2 Mix together the fresh and canned tomatoes, sugar, and vinegar. Season with salt and pepper, and stir to mix evenly.

3 Cook the pasta in plenty of boiling salted water, according to the package instructions, until *al dente*. Drain, reserving a little of the cooking water to keep the pasta moist.

4 Meanwhile, transfer the tomato mixture into a hot frying pan over medium heat. Add the pesto ingredients. Stir for a minute or so to *just* warm through, then remove from the heat. Add to the freshly cooked pasta, tossing to blend. Toss in the arugula. Serve immediately, sprinkled with Parmesan.

Note Roasting garlic is very simple. Just put a couple of fat, unpeeled cloves on a hot griddle or ridged cast-iron grill pan. Char-grill for a few minutes on each side until soft inside. Allow to cool, peel, and use the roasted pulp in the recipe.

Hillbilly Potato Leaf (p53)

Works well with
Beefsteak (pp52–63)
Standard globe (pp22–35)

Chutneys

The first of this spicy duo is a fresh Hyderabadi chutney that is at its best when eaten right away. *Pimentón* and roasted red peppers add smoky piquancy to the second, which only improves over time.

Makes about 2¼lb (1 kg)
Prep time: 15 minutes
Cooking time: 20 minutes

2lb (800g) cherry tomatoes
1 tsp chili powder
1 tsp ground turmeric
2 garlic cloves, crushed to
  a paste with a little salt
½ cup vegetable oil, plus 3 tbsp
2 tsp cumin seeds
3 dried red chiles
10 fresh or frozen curry leaves
  (available at Indian markets)

Savi's fresh tomato chutney (pictured)

Put the tomatoes, chili powder, turmeric, and garlic in a large stainless steel saucepan over medium heat. Bring to a simmer, and cook until the liquid evaporates—about 10 minutes. Add the ½ cup oil to the pan, and continue cooking until the oil rises to the top. Next, temper the spices by heating the extra oil in a small pan or wok over medium-high heat. When the oil is hot, add the cumin seeds, then the chiles, and finally the curry leaves. Once the chiles have turned dark red, empty the contents of the pan into the tomato chutney. Mix well. Be careful, as the spices can burn very quickly. Serve as part of an Indian meal or just as an excuse to spice up most things. It will keep in the refrigerator for up to 1 week.

Makes about 3lb (1.5 kg)
Prep time: 40 minutes
Cooking time: 1–1½ hours

2¼lb (1kg) ripe tomatoes,
  peeled, cored, and roughly
  chopped
1 large (9oz/250g) onion,
  roughly chopped
2 sweet red bell peppers,
  roasted, skinned, and
  coarsely chopped
⅔ cup demerara (raw) sugar
2 tsp salt
1 tsp pimentón picante
  (Spanish hot smoked paprika)
1¼ cups red wine vinegar

Tomato chutney with pimentón and red peppers

Put all the ingredients, except for the vinegar, in a large stainless steel saucepan. Cook over medium heat until the sugar starts to dissolve and coats the rest of the ingredients. Add the vinegar, and bring to a boil. Reduce the heat to a gentle simmer and cook for 1–1½ hours, stirring from time to time, until the onions and peppers are very soft and the chutney is thick. Ladle into hot, sterilized jars with tight-fitting lids, seal straight away, and label (pp142–143). This chutney is perfect with grilled meats. Its flavors improve if allowed to mature before opening, and it will keep for up to 9 months when stored in a cool, dark place.

Gazpacho

Ideal for when you have a glut of tomatoes on your hands, the truly great thing about gazpacho is how easy it is to make. The only thing you need for an irresistible result is good-quality ingredients—they really do make all the difference to this refreshing chilled soup.

Serves 4
Prep time: about 20 minutes
Cooking time: 5–7 minutes
Chilling time: 2 hours

4 large ripe beefsteak
   tomatoes, about 2¼lb
   (1kg), peeled, quartered,
   and seeded

3 tbsp extra virgin olive oil

1 tbsp sherry vinegar, cider
   vinegar, or apple vinegar

1 tbsp crumbled chicken or
   vegetable bouillon cubes

2 green bell peppers, seeded
   and finely diced

1 large cucumber or 2 Lebanese
   cucumbers, peeled, seeded,
   and finely diced

sea salt and freshly ground
   black pepper

To serve

garlic croutons (see cook's tip)

2 hard-boiled eggs, diced
   (optional)

1 Put the tomatoes in a blender with 2 tbsp water, and blend to a very smooth pulp. Transfer the pulpy liquid to a heavy saucepan and cook gently for 2–3 minutes.

2 Add the olive oil, vinegar, crumbled bouillon, peppers, and diced cucumber. Cook over medium heat for 3–4 minutes until just below the boiling point, stirring from time to time. Remove from the heat, and allow to cool.

3 Once the soup has cooled to room temperature, season very well with salt and pepper; don't scrimp on the seasoning. Pour the soup into a large bowl and chill in the refrigerator for a few hours until cold. Taste and season again if needed.

4 Serve the gazpacho chilled, garnished with garlic croutons and diced hard-boiled egg (if using).

Note It is important that your gazpacho is well seasoned—almost too generously. Since it is going to be eaten cold, it needs to be very tasty. Remember, the flavors in cold food do not come through as strongly as they do in food that is served hot or at room temperature.

Cook's tip To make garlic croutons, rub some day-old bread with the cut side of a garlic clove. Cut into small cubes, toss in a little olive oil, and sprinkle with sea salt. Spread out on a baking sheet, and roast in a preheated 350°F (180°C) oven for 10 minutes, or until crisp and golden.

Works well with
Beefsteak (pp52–63)
Plum (pp64–73)

Simple marinara-style sauce for pizza

The name *marinara* comes not from its contents, but from its origins as a favorite choice of hungry fishermen in Naples. Returning to port after a long night at sea, they would reportedly slather the sauce over rounds of flat bread. All those healthy appetites can't be wrong ...

**Makes enough for
2 medium pizzas
Prep time: 10 minutes
Cooking time: 25 minutes**

5 ripe tomatoes, about
    1lb (450g), peeled
    and chopped

2 tbsp extra virgin olive oil

2 garlic cloves, crushed

½ tsp dried oregano

1 tbsp capers in brine,
    rinsed, gently squeezed dry,
    and finely chopped

2 tbsp coarsely chopped
    flat-leaf parsley

1 Put all the ingredients except for the parsley in a saucepan, and simmer over low heat for about 5 minutes, or until the tomatoes appear watery. Cook, covered, for about 15 minutes, until the tomatoes and garlic are soft. Add the parsley, and cook for 5 minutes longer.

2 Remove from the heat and allow to cool. Spread onto your pizza as a base for other toppings of your choice. Or, if you want to serve your pizza in the classic marinara style, simply spread the pizza dough with the sauce, scatter a little slivered garlic and a sprinkling of oregano over the top, drizzle over some extra virgin olive oil, and bake. And there you have it—a version of the original pizza topping so beloved by Neapolitans.

Note Why not make a batch of this sauce and freeze it to use later? After cooking the tomatoes and garlic in step 1, pour the sauce into a zipper-seal plastic bag and freeze (p143).

Works well with
Plum (pp64–73)
Beefsteak (pp52–63)
Standard globe (pp22–35)

Salsas

Salsa de molcajete has a wonderful smoky flavor from the char-grilling, while *Pico de gallo*, which literally means "rooster's beak," is the mother of all Mexican salsas with its fresh simplicity.

Makes about 1½ cups
Prep time: 10 minutes
Cooking time: 10 minutes

6 plum tomatoes or
    4 beefsteak tomatoes
2 fresh green bird's-eye hot
    chiles, stemmed and chopped
½ small red onion, finely
    chopped
3 tbsp finely chopped cilantro
    (use leaves and stems)
juice of 1 lime
sea salt

Salsa de Molcajete (pictured)

Put the tomatoes and chiles on a very hot griddle or under the broiler, and turn to blacken on all sides. Let cool for about 5 minutes. On a wooden cutting board, cut the tomatoes into quarters, then scrape into a food processor with their seeds and any juice. Add the chiles, and process for about 30 seconds until you have a coarse-textured purée. Alternatively, pound the tomatoes and chiles using a large mortar and pestle. Transfer to a serving bowl and add the onion, cilantro, and lime juice. Season generously with salt. Taste, and adjust as needed – remember, seasoning is key, so don't scrimp. Let stand for 1 hour to allow the flavors to develop. This salsa also keeps very well for a couple of days if stored, covered, in the refrigerator. Serve at room temperature with tacos, fajitas, or char-grilled meats.

Makes about 1½ cups
Prep time: 10 minutes

6 plum tomatoes, seeded and
    finely chopped
1 white onion, finely chopped
1 ripe avocado (optional)
3 tbsp finely chopped cilantro
    (use both leaves and stems)
1–2 fresh green thai, bird's-eye,
    or serrano hot chiles, seeded
    and finely chopped
juice of 1 lime
sea salt

Pico de gallo

Put the tomatoes and onion in a bowl. Halve and pit the avocado (if using), and cut into dice. Add to the bowl with the cilantro and stir through gently. Next, add the chile a little at a time, tasting as you go, and stop when you reach the desired level of heat. Season with a little salt, and squeeze in the fresh lime juice. Serve immediately with freshly made tortillas, in tacos or fajitas, or alongside steaks marinated with lime juice and a little olive oil.

Variation Stir some sweetcorn kernels or cooked black beans into the salsa just before serving.

Roasted tomato and garlic soup

This soup is simple to make and has deliciously satisfying results. If you like, roast the vegetables in advance, and refrigerate them for 2–3 days until needed. The really good news is that, once this is done, the soup takes only 5 minutes to prepare. Homemade food in a jiffy.

Serves 4
Prep time: 15 minutes
Cooking time: 30 minutes

8 plum tomatoes, about 1½lb (675g), quartered

1 red onion, cut into 8 wedges

2 unpeeled garlic cloves

3 tbsp olive oil

4 cups hot vegetable stock

3 tbsp sun-dried tomato paste (available in tubes at many well-stocked supermarkets)

sea salt and freshly ground black pepper

1 To roast the vegetables, heat the oven to 350°F (180°C). Put the tomatoes, onion, and garlic on a large parchment-lined baking sheet. Drizzle with olive oil and season well with salt and pepper. Roast, turning once or twice, until all the vegetables are soft, caramelized, and lightly browned—allow 10–15 minutes for the garlic, 15–20 minutes for the onion, and 25 minutes for the tomatoes. Squeeze the garlic from the skin once it has cooled slightly.

2 Using a hand-held blender, process together the vegetable stock, sun-dried tomato paste, and roasted vegetables until a chunky purée forms. Adjust the seasoning as needed and reheat gently. Serve hot.

Variations Try adding a dollop of mascarpone cheese, croutons, or roasted cumin seeds to each serving. Or vary the soup recipe itself by adding some chopped fresh herbs such as thyme, basil, or rosemary.

Works well with
Plum (pp64–73)
Cherry (pp36–51)

Sofrito

Sofrito, sofrigit, soffritto, refogado—this basic sauce pops up in Spanish, Latin American, Italian, Portuguese, and Sephardic cuisine. There are countless variations, and each cuisine has its particular stamp—onion, garlic, and tomatoes are used in Spain, for instance.

Makes about 1¼ cups
Prep time: 5 minutes
Cooking time: 25 minutes

Basic sofrito

1–2 tbsp good-quality olive oil

1 onion, finely chopped or thinly sliced

1–2 garlic cloves, finely chopped or pounded to a paste using a mortar and pestle

4 ripe plum tomatoes, about 10–12oz (300–360g), chopped (peeled and seeded, or not, according to taste)

1 Heat the oil in a medium frying pan. Add the onion and cook gently for 5–10 minutes, stirring from time to time with a wooden spoon, until golden brown. Add the garlic and cook for 1 minute, stirring constantly.

2 Add the tomatoes and cook over medium heat, stirring occasionally. As the tomatoes cook down, the sauce becomes syrupy and rich. Depending on the type of dish you are making, you may need to cook longer to thicken.

3 At this point, the basic sofrito is ready. You can now add a variety of herbs, spices, meat, fish, or wine, then continue with your dish. Below are some suggestions.

Variations

• Seed a dried ancho or chipotle chile and cover with hot water. Purée the chile and its soaking liquid into a paste. Add to the sofrito to make a Mexican salsa for meatballs or to use for dishes such as chili con carne.

• Add a glass of good red wine and some fresh herbs such as rosemary or oregano, to use with pork or lamb.

• Soften a few saffron threads in ⅓ cup water. Add to the sofrito and cook until slightly thickened. Use with pasta shapes such as orzo, fregola, and malloredus.

• Add ½ tsp pimentón (Spanish smoked paprika) and freshly squeezed orange juice to make a great sauce for white fish.

Works well with
Plum (pp64–73)
Standard globe (pp22–35)

Ketchup ... of course

A book on tomatoes would not be complete without ketchup, so here is a recipe for classic tomato ketchup, in trademark red, with a green tomato variation, which is great for using up lots of unripe tomatoes.

Makes about 4½lb (2kg)
Prep time: 40 minutes
Cooking time: 2 hours

4½lb (2kg) ripe plum tomatoes, peeled and coarsely chopped

1lb (500g) Granny Smith or other cooking apples, peeled, cored, and chopped

3 onions, chopped

¾ cup granulated sugar

⅓ cup dark brown sugar

2 cups cider vinegar

1 tbsp salt

½ tsp chili powder

½ tsp ground cinnamon

½ tsp freshly ground black pepper

8 whole allspice berries

7 whole cloves

Red tomato ketchup (pictured)

Combine all the ingredients in a large stainless steel pan. Bring to a boil, then reduce the heat slightly. Simmer, uncovered, for 2 hours, stirring from time to time. Remove from the heat and allow to cool slightly. Using a hand-held blender, purée the mixture until velvety smooth. If the sauce is still watery, simmer for another 20–30 minutes, until thick and a rich reddish brown, stirring constantly. Pass the ketchup through a sieve, and ladle into hot sterilized jars or bottles. Seal tightly with nonreactive lids straight away, label, and store in a cool, dark place. It keeps for up to 9 months.

Green tomato ketchup

Use either unripe tomatoes or green varieties such as 'Green Zebra' (p26) for this variation, and perhaps even a few tomatillos (papery husks removed). You will end up with about 2¼lb (1kg) ketchup. Put 3lb (1.5kg) cored and quartered unripe or green tomatoes, 1lb (500g) Granny Smith or other cooking apples, peeled, cored, and cut into small dice, and 1 large chopped onion in a large stainless steel pan. Add 1 cinnamon stick, 6 allspice berries, 4 cloves, ½ tsp cayenne pepper, 1 tsp black peppercorns, 1 bay leaf, 1 tbsp salt, and 1¼ cups cider vinegar. Bring to a boil and cook for 20 minutes or until the fruit and vegetables soften. Add 1 cup demerara sugar, dissolve completely, then bring to a gentle simmer. Cook for 1 hour, uncovered, until very soft and thick, stirring from time to time. Blend to a smooth purée, then pass through a sieve back into the pan. Simmer for another 20–30 minutes until the ketchup is thick. Ladle into sterilized jars or bottles, seal, and store as above. It keeps for up to 6 months.

Tomato and Gruyère tart

The flavors of tomatoes and Gruyère combine perfectly. Gruyère also pairs beautifully with white wine, so the white wine in the pastry makes this tart a good combination altogether.

Serves 8
Prep time: 30 minutes plus 30 minutes for chilling
Cooking time: 45 minutes

For the pastry

2 cups all-purpose flour

pinch of salt

7 tbsp cold butter, cut into cubes

1½ tbsp cold or frozen lard or vegetable shortening

1 egg

4 tbsp cold dry white wine

For the filling

1 cup heavy cream

8oz (200g) Gruyère cheese, grated

1¾oz (50g) plain oatcakes, crushed into crumbs (about ½ cup)

about 1¾lb (800g) ripe tomatoes, halved and seeded

½ tsp dried thyme or oregano

freshly ground black pepper

1 To make the pastry, process the flour, butter, lard, and salt in a food processor for 20 seconds, or until the mixture resembles breadcrumbs, then add the egg. With the machine running, add the wine a little at a time, just until the dough comes together. With your hands, quickly work into a disk about 1in (2.5cm) thick. Wrap in plastic wrap and chill for 30 minutes.

2 Preheat the oven to 350F° (180°C).

3 On a floured work surface, roll the pastry until about ¼in (5mm) thick. Use to line a 10in (25cm) tart pan with a removable bottom. Prick the base with a fork and line the pan with baking parchment. Fill with ceramic pie weights or uncooked beans, and bake for 10 minutes. Remove the paper and beans, and bake the pastry for another 5 minutes.

4 Spread the oatcake crumbs over the bottom of the pastry shell, and top with the tomatoes. Sprinkle with thyme or oregano, and season with salt and black pepper. Scatter the cheese over the top; then pour in the cream.

5 Bake in the middle of the oven for 30 minutes or until the tart looks brown all over. Let cool slightly before removing the ring from the pan. Serve hot or cold with a salad.

Loveheart (p41)

Works well with
Cherry (pp36–51)
Standard globe (pp22–35)

Basil and Parmesan stuffed tomatoes

It simply had to be: a recipe for this culinary stalwart of tomato cuisine. These are great served on their own or even grilled in their foil parcels as part of a barbecue. Remember, always use fresh herbs.

Makes 1 large stuffed tomato*
Prep time: 25 minutes
Baking time: 30 minutes

1 large beefsteak tomato, about 8–10oz (250–280g)
1 large egg, beaten
1 tbsp fresh white breadcrumbs
1 tbsp olive oil
½ tsp sugar

Basil and Parmesan filling

2 tbsp shredded basil leaves
1 tbsp finely chopped flat-leaf parsley
1 tbsp finely chopped rinsed and drained capers
1 tbsp freshly grated Parmesan cheese
½ tsp freshly grated lemon zest
salt and freshly ground black pepper
pinch of sugar
salt and freshly ground black pepper

* It is easy to make this recipe for more people. Simply adjust the amounts according to how many tomatoes you are using and how large they are.

1 Preheat the oven to 350°F (180°C). Carefully slice the top off the tomato to make a lid. Core and scoop out the insides, removing the seeds and jellylike juice (p138). Put the tomato shell and its lid cut-side down in a colander.

2 To make the filling, mix together the basil, parsley, capers, Parmesan, and lemon zest. Season generously with salt and pepper, taste, and adjust the seasoning if needed. Combine with the beaten egg and breadcrumbs. Fill the tomato shell until it is well stuffed, cover with its lid, and place right-side up in a baking dish lined with a piece of foil.

3 In a small bowl, mix together the oil, sugar, and 2 tbsp water. Pour over the tomato, and enclose in the foil to make a parcel. Bake in the middle of the oven for 30 minutes or until soft and gooey. Serve on its own, accompanied by a peppery salad of arugula and watercress, or as a side dish.

Variations Use 1 tbsp coarsely chopped tarragon, 1 tbsp finely chopped flat-leaf parsley, 1 tbsp finely chopped rinsed and drained capers, 2 tsp freshly grated lemon zest, and 1 tbsp half and half for the filling. Season, and make as above. Or try mixing the scooped-out flesh, seeds, and jellylike juice with 1 tbsp chopped dill, 1 tbsp shredded mint leaves, 1 tbsp finely chopped onion or shallot, 1 tbsp chopped toasted pine nuts, 1 tsp freshly squeezed lemon juice, 1 tbsp olive oil, and a pinch of sugar. Mix together, season, and make as above. For an extra, meaty dimension to the second filling, add some sautéed ground lamb.

Work well with
Beefsteak (pp52–63)
Standard globe (pp22–35)

Ragù bolognese

This unashamedly tomato-heavy interpretation of the classic *ragù bolognese* comes from Marine Ices, a London culinary institution. Long, slow simmering brings out the rich flavor of the tomatoes. Thank you, Marine Ices.

Serves 8
Prep time: 45 minutes
Cooking time: at least 2 hours

1 tbsp olive oil
1 onion, finely chopped
2 celery ribs, finely chopped
2 carrots, finely diced
2lb (1kg) 90% lean ground beef
½ cup dry red wine
6½lb (3kg) ripe plum tomatoes, peeled and chopped
1 x (6oz) can tomato paste
1 bay leaf
freshly grated nutmeg, to taste
1 tbsp butter
salt and freshly ground black pepper

1 Heat the oil in a very large saucepan, and stir in the onions, celery, and carrots. Cook gently for 5–10 minutes, until soft but not browned. This initial technique is an example of an Italian *soffritto* (p157).

2 Add the ground beef and cook until the meat is well browned, stirring constantly and breaking up any large chunks of meat with a wooden spoon.

3 Pour in the red wine, then stir in the tomatoes, tomato paste, and bay leaf. Bring almost to a boil. Reduce the heat and gently simmer the ragù for at least 2 hours, stirring from time to time, until well reduced to a nice thick sauce.

4 Season well with a good pinch of nutmeg, salt, and pepper. Taste, adjusting the seasoning if needed, then stir in the butter. Serve hot with pasta or use as a sauce for lasagna.

Note The time spent peeling the tomatoes for this recipe may seem a little daunting—but persevere. Your efforts will be well rewarded in the delicious end result.

Works well with
Plum (pp64–73)

Mexican-style tomato summer pudding

Make this sort of treasure chest brimming with an assortment of tasty tomatoes—green, yellow, red, quartered plum tomatoes, long slices of beefsteaks, tomato wedges, and even whole cherry tomatoes.

Serves 4
Prep time: 30 minutes
Soaking time: overnight

1 small loaf sliced white bread, crusts removed (about 2lb/700g)

8–9 very ripe tomatoes, about 1½lb (675g), cored and seeded (reserve the seeds and jellylike core)

2 roasted tomatoes, cut into quarters (p141)

3 sun-dried tomatoes in olive oil, chopped

¾ cup tomato juice

5 tbsp olive oil

grated zest (optional) and juice of ½ lime

large dash Maggi Liquid Seasoning

large dash soy sauce

large dash Worcestershire sauce

2 tbsp homemade or good-quality ketchup (p158)

1 fresh red bird's-eye hot chile pepper, finely chopped

4 tbsp finely chopped cilantro

1 tbsp finely chopped shallot

8oz (200g) peeled and deveined cooked prawns

sea salt and freshly ground black pepper

freshly sliced ripe avocado

1 Set 2 whole bread slices aside, and cut the rest in half. Line a 2-quart (1.5-liter) glass or ceramic bowl with the bread halves, overlapping each slice a little bit.

2 Cut the fresh tomatoes into random shapes—peel some, leave others unpeeled, and keep small ones whole. Set aside with the roasted and sun-dried tomatoes.

3 Blend or process the reserved seeds and "jelly" to a purée, and put in a small pitcher or glass measuring cup. Add the remaining ingredients, except for the prawns and avocado. Do this little by little, tasting as you go. The flavor should be strong but not overpowering. Season with salt and pepper.

4 Mix the prepared tomatoes and prawns together, and use to fill the bread bowl—the filling should come three-quarters of the way up the sides. Pour in half of the spicy juice mixture until the tomatoes are covered. Use the reserved 2 whole slices of bread to cover the top. Carefully pour in the remaining juice mixture, place a saucer directly on top of the bread, weigh down with cans of food, and chill overnight.

5 To serve, turn the bowl upside down onto a large plate. Carefully lift the bowl so that the pudding breaks open and people can help themselves. Serve with the avocado slices.

Yellow Butterfly (p68)

Works well with
All tomatoes (pp22–77)

Baked beans

If you're looking for inspiration, try this dish. It takes a little planning, as you need to soak the beans overnight, but after that everything is simply put together and baked. Once you have tasted these, you will realize exactly how good homemade baked beans really are.

Serves 4
Soaking time: overnight
Prep time: 20 minutes
Cooking time: 2–3 hours

1 cup small dried white beans
1 tbsp vegetable oil
1 onion, finely chopped
2 garlic cloves, finely minced
1 tbsp black treacle or
  unsulphered molasses
1 tbsp maple syrup
½ tsp ground cumin
¼ tsp ground cinnamon
¼ tsp cayenne pepper
5 large tomatoes, about
  1lb (450g), peeled
  and chopped
1 tbsp very finely chopped
  sun-dried tomatoes
1 tbsp tomato paste
1 tsp English mustard powder,
  such as Colman's
sea salt and freshly ground
  black pepper

1 Put the beans in a large bowl and cover with plenty of cold water—enough to cover by at least 2in (4cm). Let soak overnight.

2 Drain and rinse the soaked beans. Put in a large heavy pan, cover with plenty of fresh cold water, and bring to a boil. Boil rapidly for 10 minutes, reduce the heat slightly, and simmer for 1 hour; drain.

3 Preheat the oven to 275°F (140°C). Put the beans in a flameproof casserole with the remaining ingredients, except for the salt (this is important—adding salt at this point would toughen the beans). Season with a good grinding of pepper, and add 2 cups cold water.

4 Gently bring to a boil, cover, and transfer the casserole to the oven. Bake for about 4 hours, stirring from time to time. Keep an eye on the beans as they cook; if the mixture is too thick or starting to dry out, add a little water as needed. Once the beans are creamy and soft, add enough salt to season well. Bake for 5 minutes longer, then serve.

Variation To cook the beans without baking, follow steps 1 and 2, then put the beans in a clean pan with the rest of the ingredients, except the salt. Season with pepper, and bring to a boil. Reduce the heat slightly, cover, and simmer very gently, stirring from time to time, for 1–2 hours or until the beans are tender. Season well with salt, and serve.

Works well with
Plum (pp64–73)
Standard globe (pp22–35)

Slow-cooked beef cheeks with braised vegetables

Arte Culinaria is a fantastic cooking school in Italy's Veneto region, and its hostess, Antonella Tagliapietra, is the source of this wonderful dish. A classic example of slow cooking, it uses a cut of meat that is often overlooked—yet truly mouthwatering and meltingly tender.

Serves 4
Prep time: 20 minutes
Cooking time: 3 hours

3 tbsp olive oil

2 onions, chopped

1½lb (700g) beef cheeks, cut into chunks and trimmed of any fat

1 bay leaf

sprig of fresh rosemary

⅔ cup dry white wine

2 large carrots, thickly sliced

1 celery root, peeled, quartered, and sliced

6–7 very ripe tomatoes, about 1lb (500g), peeled and chopped

1 tsp salt

1 Heat the oil over medium-high heat in a large heavy pan such as an enameled cast-iron saucepan or casserole. Cook the onions, stirring occasionally, until they begin to turn golden brown, 7–9 minutes.

2 Add the beef cheeks, bay leaf, and rosemary to the onions, and continue to cook, stirring occasionally, until the meat is browned on all sides. When the meat begins to stick to the bottom of the pan, add the wine and stir to deglaze and scrape up any browned bits.

3 Stir in the carrots, celery root, tomatoes, salt, and 1 cup water. Reduce the heat to low and simmer very gently, uncovered, for 2½ hours or until tender. Stir from time to time, so the meat does not stick to the bottom; add a little extra wine or water if the mixture becomes too dry.

4 Serve hot with polenta.

Variation Beef shoulder and chuck are also good choices for this recipe. You could also try it with cuts of lamb that benefit from long, slow cooking.

Works well with
Plum (pp64–73)
Standard globe (pp22–35)

Tomato panade

This is a baked combination of the traditional French soup *panade*, usually eaten as a thick bready broth with caramelized onions, and the Italian *pappa al pomodoro*, another bready broth, but with tomatoes.

**Serves 6 as a main course
or 8 as a side dish
Prep time: 40 minutes
Cooking time: 40 minutes**

3 large onions, thinly sliced

about 2 tbsp olive oil, plus extra for drizzling

8 garlic cloves, coarsely chopped and crushed to a paste with a little salt

½ fresh red chile pepper, seeded and very finely chopped

4 ripe plum tomatoes, about 10–12oz (300–360g), coarsely chopped, or 1 x 14oz (400g) can whole peeled plum tomatoes, coarsely chopped

1 x 14oz (400g) baguette, cut into slices ¼in (5mm) thick

handful of fresh basil leaves, coarsely torn

6 large, ripe round tomatoes, or 2–3 beefsteak tomatoes, about 1¼lb (550g), cut into ¼in (5mm) slices

¼ cup freshly grated Parmesan cheese

4oz (125g) sliced mozzarella cheese

1¼ cups hot chicken stock

sea salt and freshly ground black pepper

1 Preheat the oven to 350°F (180°C).

2 Heat about 2 tbsp olive oil in a large frying pan over medium heat. Gently cook the onions for 10–15 minutes until they are just beginning to brown. Add the garlic paste and chile and cook for 10–15 minutes longer, stirring frequently, until the onions are nicely browned. Add in the chopped tomatoes, adding a little water if the mixture is too dry; if using canned tomatoes, add the entire contents of the can, juice and all. Season with salt and pepper.

3 Oil a 2-quart (2-liter) baking dish. Line the bottom of the dish with half of the baguette slices, arranged closely together. Sprinkle with a little olive oil, then spread half of the onion and tomato mixture over the top. Layer with half of the sliced tomatoes, and top with half of the basil leaves. Sprinkle with half of the Parmesan. Repeat the layering process, finishing with the remaining Parmesan. Top with the mozzarella slices, and drizzle the stock over the top.

4 Bake in the middle of the oven for 40–45 minutes or until the top is crusty and golden. Remove from the oven, and let cool for 5 minutes before serving. Serve with salad, grilled asparagus, and perhaps some lemony grilled chicken.

Pink Accordion (p55)

Works well with
Beefsteak (pp52–63)
Plum (pp64–73)
Standard globe (pp22–35)

Melted feta on tomatoes and spinach

This is a truly scrumptious salad, where hot oil is poured over feta cheese, which in turn melts to drizzle the tomatoes and spinach with moist and oily juices, which then create their own dressing.

Serves 4 as a starter
Prep time: 15 minutes

2½ cups fresh baby spinach leaves, rinsed and dried

12 oil-packed kalamata olives, pitted

1 tbsp capers in brine, rinsed, drained, and gently squeezed dry

8 sun-dried tomato halves packed in olive oil, coarsely chopped

1 shallot, finely chopped

2 large beefsteak tomatoes, about 550g (1¼lb), sliced

4oz (100g) feta cheese

⅓ cup olive oil

2 tbsp sherry vinegar or red wine vinegar

freshly ground black pepper

garlic croutons, to serve (optional) (p152)

1 In a large salad bowl, gently toss together the spinach, olives, capers, sun-dried tomatoes, and shallot. Layer the tomatoes on top of the salad, and crumble the feta on top.

2 Heat the olive oil in a small heavy pan until quite hot, then drizzle carefully over the salad. Sprinkle with the vinegar and season with a good grinding of black pepper. Serve at once, topped with the croutons (if using) or accompanied by some garlicky country-style bread.

A word of warning: To avoid splattering, make sure the ingredients are dry before adding the oil. Spin-dry the spinach well; once you have added the tomatoes to the salad, you may need to pat them dry with paper towels before pouring in the oil. If you are worried about pouring the oil directly into your salad bowl, use a wok instead.

Stupice (p27)

Works well with
Beefsteak (pp52–63)
Standard globe (p22–35)
Plum (pp64–73)

Pan-fried marrow and green tomatoes

Perfect for when your garden is producing at its peak and you are awash in a glut of fresh vegetables, this recipe uses summer squash, but zucchini or pumpkin also work well. Unripe tomatoes provide the perfect complement, while pimentón adds a deliciously rich kick.

Serves 6
Prep time: 20 minutes
Cooking time: 15 minutes

2 tbsp butter

2 tbsp olive oil, as needed

2 onions, sliced

2¼lb (1kg) summer squash, halved, peeled, and seeded if needed, and cut into ½in (1cm) slices

8 unripe tomatoes, about 1¼–1½lb (650–675g), halved and sliced

1 tsp pimentón (Spanish smoked paprika), or to taste

juice of 2 oranges (about ⅔ cup)

sea salt and freshly ground black pepper

1 In a frying pan, melt the butter over medium heat. Cook the onions for about 10 minutes, stirring occasionally, until they are very soft and brown.

2 Add the squash slices and cook on both sides for about 10 minutes or until quite soft. If the mixture becomes too dry, add a little of the olive oil. Add the tomato slices, and cook for 2–3 minutes. Sprinkle in the pimentón, and season with salt and pepper.

3 To finish, increase the heat slightly and add the orange juice, a little at a time, stirring to release any browned bits from the bottom of the pan. Let cook for a couple of minutes until thickened to a saucelike consistency. Serve hot as a breakfast dish with eggs and bacon, or for an outdoor brunch.

Works well with
Standard globe (pp22–35)
Beefsteak (pp52–63)
Plum (pp64–73)

Tomato salad with tarragon, lemon zest, and capers

People often bemoan the fact that today's tomatoes are tasteless. Well, a good thing about working with something that is arguably not very tasty is that it can act as a sponge for other, stronger flavors. If you do have flavorful tomatoes on hand, that can only be a bonus.

Serves 4
Prep time: 20 minutes

6 ripe tomatoes, about 1lb (450g), peeled, seeded, and cut into strips

2 tbsp coarsely chopped tarragon

2 tbsp capers in brine, drained, rinsed, and finely chopped

2 tsp grated lemon zest

2 tbsp extra virgin olive oil, or more to taste

1 Mix together all the ingredients in a glass or ceramic bowl.

2 Let stand for 10 minutes to allow the flavors to blend, then serve as a side salad. This works particularly well with grilled fish or chicken.

Works well with
Beefsteak (pp52–63)
Plum (pp64–73)

Tomato, peach, and strawberry salad

Fruit salad with a twist! Fresh and zinging with flavor, it is also a visual feast. Even if its fruits come into season at different times in your garden, depending on variety and where you live, you may still be able to catch them all at the same time. If you can't, go shopping.

Serves 4
Prep time: 10 minutes

4–6 ripe tomatoes, about 12oz–1lb (350–450g)

3 ripe peaches

15 strawberries

dash of extra virgin olive oil

dash of balsamic vinegar

handful of fresh mint leaves, shredded

sea salt and freshly ground black pepper

1 Cut the tomatoes in half. (If using cherry tomatoes, cut them into halves or quarters, if large.) Halve and pit the peaches, and cut into wedges. Halve the strawberries, discarding the hulls.

2 Put the tomatoes, peaches, and strawberries in a glass or ceramic serving dish. Add olive oil and balsamic vinegar. Season with salt and plenty of black pepper, and add the shredded mint. Toss gently until the fruit is evenly coated with the dressing. Serve immediately.

Jelly Bean (p40)

Works well with
All tomatoes (pp22–77)

Fresh tomatoes marinated with garlic

Particularly delicious on a hot summer's day, there really could be nothing simpler. The secrets to success are using only the choicest ingredients and allowing time for the flavors to blend. The salt draws out moisture from the tomatoes, creating their own tempting dressing.

Serves 4
Prep time: 10 minutes
Marinating time: 2 hours

4 large beefsteak
    tomatoes, about 2½lb
    (1.1kg), sliced
1 or 2 garlic cloves
¼ cup extra virgin olive oil
1–2 tbsp good-quality
    sherry vinegar
handful of fresh basil leaves,
    shredded (optional)
sea salt and freshly ground
    black pepper

1 Put the tomatoes in a shallow glass or ceramic dish.

2 Using a mortar and pestle, pound the garlic with a little sea salt to form a paste. Add to the tomatoes, along with the oil and vinegar. Season generously with a good sprinkling of salt and pepper. Gently mix well so that all the ingredients are evenly dispersed. Let stand in a cool part of the kitchen for 2 hours.

3 Serve at room temperature—this is important—as an accompaniment to grilled meat or fish, or as a side salad for lunch, topped with the shredded basil (if using). Make sure there is plenty of fresh, crusty bread on the table to soak up the delicious juices.

Variation If you like, use any other fresh herb to top the marinated salad—try rosemary, oregano, thyme, flat-leaf parsley, or tarragon.

Works well with
Beefsteak (pp52–63)
Plum (pp64–73)
Standard globe (pp22–35)

Dressings

With their intrinsic acidity, tomatoes are a good ingredient for salad dressings. Next time you are using tomatoes and are about to discard the juicy inside and its seeds, think about keeping this to use as a partial substitute for vinegar or lemon juice in a dressing.

Makes enough to dress a salad for 4
Prep time: 10 minutes

Proportions for basic dressing

2 tbsp sieved tomato juices (see step 1)

2 tbsp good-quality extra virgin olive oil

2 tsp vinegar such as apple cider vinegar or balsamic vinegar

sea salt and freshly ground black pepper to taste

1 Here is a rough guide to preparing a tomato-based dressing: adjust the amounts up and down accordingly, to make the amount you need. First, core and seed a juicy tomato—plum, cherry, and standard globe tomatoes are best for this. Keep the seeds plus any juices, and blend or process until smooth. Pass through a fine sieve if you like.

2 To this mixture, add an equal amount (by volume) of good-quality extra virgin olive oil and a little vinegar. Season with salt and pepper. Whisk with a fork, taste, and adjust the flavors to suit you. And there you have it—a simple yet tasty dressing ready to drizzle over your favorite salad.

Variations

- Some chopped fresh dill and a little freshly toasted and ground cumin seeds transform this dressing into something delicious for roasted tomato, carrot, and beet salads.

- Add some finely sliced fresh basil leaves and freshly puréed garlic (use a mortar and pestle to crush the garlic with a little salt) to the basic dressing, and use balsamic vinegar—perfect for summery tomato salads.

- For a piquant dressing with a Spanish touch, add a pinch or so of pimentón (Spanish smoked paprika), and use freshly squeezed orange or lemon juice, or both, instead of vinegar. This is ideal for a red pepper, tomato, and orange salad.

Works well with
Plum (pp64–73)
Cherry (pp36–51)
Standard globe (pp22–35)

Turkish shepherd's salad

A beautiful combination of colors and contrasting flavors and textures, this wonderful wintry salad is a definite treat during the chilly months of the year. It can also be made 2–3 hours in advance. Simply prepare the salad, then leave it in a cool place until needed.

Serves 6
Prep time: 20 minutes

¼ red cabbage, about 7oz (200g), quartered and very thinly sliced

5 tbsp extra virgin olive oil

juice of 1 lemon, or to taste

sumac or zahtar, to taste

5 large ripe tomatoes, about 1lb (450g), cut into wedges and preferably roasted (p156)

2 large roasted beets, sliced

½ red onion, very finely chopped

5 tbsp finely chopped flat-leaf parsley

3 tbsp finely chopped dill

5 tbsp fresh mint leaves, torn if large

sea salt and freshly ground black pepper

1 In a large bowl, mix together the cabbage and olive oil. Add the lemon juice, a little at a time, until you are pleased with the taste. Sprinkle the cabbage with a little sumac, and season with salt and pepper.

2 Stir well to make sure the cabbage is thoroughly coated with dressing, then add the remaining ingredients and toss again. Season generously with pepper and just a little salt—and extra sumac, if needed. Serve at cool room temperature.

Note Sumac is a berry with citrusy tones, which comes from Turkey. It is delicious in salads and with grilled meats. If you have trouble finding it, add some zahtar (available in Middle Eastern markets and many well-stocked supermarkets), or use lemon juice or red pepper flakes instead.

Floridity (p70)

Works well with
Plum (pp64–73)
Standard globe (pp22–35)

Avocado, tomato, and lime salad

Ripe, unblemished avocados and vine-ripened tomatoes are one of those culinary "marriages" that are made to go together. This simple salad focuses on using the choicest ripe ingredients. A fresh vinaigrette invigorated with lime zest makes it simply irresistible.

Serves 4 as a side dish
Prep time: 10 minutes

1 tbsp hulled unsalted pumpkin seeds

2 large ripe, unblemished avocados

4 ripe beefsteak tomatoes, about 2¼–2½lb (1–1.1kg), thinly sliced

For the lime dressing

2 tbsp extra virgin olive oil

1 tbsp white wine vinegar

1 tsp tequila (optional)

grated zest and juice of ½ lime

sea salt and freshly ground black pepper

1 In a small dry frying pan over medium heat, toast the pumpkin seeds for a couple of minutes, stirring occasionally, until they start to pop, being careful not to burn them. Turn into a small bowl, and set aside.

2 To make the dressing, whisk together the oil, vinegar, tequila (if using), lime zest, and a squirt of lime juice in a small bowl. Season with salt and pepper. Taste, and adjust the seasoning if needed.

3 Halve, peel, and pit the avocados, and cut into slices lengthwise. Arrange alternating layers of avocado and tomato slices on a serving dish or platter, and drizzle the vinaigrette over the top. Scatter with the reserved toasted pumpkin seeds, and serve immediately.

Works well with
Beefsteak (pp52–63)
Cherry (pp36–51)

Caponata

One of Sicily's signature dishes, caponata's combination of sweet and sour flavors is typical of the island's distinctive cuisine. Great served with fresh crusty bread as an antipasto, it also makes an excellent side dish. As a bonus, it keeps well in the refrigerator for 3–4 days.

Serves 4 as a side dish
Prep time: 15 minutes
Cooking time: 25–30 minutes

⅓ cup olive oil

3 eggplants, cut into 1in (2cm) cubes

2 onions, sliced

½ cup finely chopped celery root or celery,

½ cup green olives in brine, pitted

¼ cup capers in brine, drained, rinsed, and gently squeezed dry

1 x 14½oz (400g) can chopped plum tomatoes, drained, or 5–6 ripe plum tomatoes, about 1½lb (550g), peeled

¼ cup sugar

¼ cup cider vinegar or white wine vinegar

¼ tsp unsweetened cocoa powder or dark chocolate (at least 70% cocoa solids), finely grated

sea salt and freshly ground black pepper

freshly chopped flat-leaf parsley, to serve

1 Heat 4 tbsp of the olive oil in a heavy frying pan over high heat. Add the eggplants and cook for 8–10 minutes, stirring occasionally, until the cubes begin to turn golden brown. Remove from the pan with a slotted spoon, and let drain on paper towels.

2 In the same pan, heat the remaining oil and cook the onions for 8–10 minutes, or until golden brown.

3 Meanwhile, blanch the celery root in a small pan of rapidly boiling water for 1 minute. When the celery root or celery is nearly cooked, turn into a colander, and refresh with cold water. Drain again.

4 Add the celery root to the sautéed onions along with the olives and capers, then add the tomatoes (or fresh tomatoes, if using), sugar, vinegar, and cocoa. Cook for 8–10 minutes over medium heat, stirring with a wooden spoon from time to time. Remove from the heat, add the reserved eggplants, and season with salt and pepper. Be careful with the amount of salt you add, as the olives and capers are already salty. Let cool to room temperature.

5 Transfer to a serving dish, and sprinkle with chopped parsley. Serve immediately.

Note If you have made the caponata ahead and stored it in a covered container in the refrigerator, return it to room temperature before serving.

Works well with
Plum (pp64–73)

Tomato and mascarpone ice cream with raspberries

The flavor of the tomatoes here may be subtle, but it is an integral and entirely delicious element of this rich and creamy concoction. Confirmation, if it was needed, that the tomato is indeed a fruit.

Makes about 1 quart (1 liter)
Prep time: 30 minutes
Freezing time: 2 hours

8oz (250g) ripe tomatoes, peeled, seeded, and finely diced (mild-tasting varieties such as yellow or vine-ripened cherry tomatoes work best)
½ cup fresh raspberries
1 tbsp granulated sugar
2 tbsp Amaretto liqueur

For the custard base
3 egg yolks
½ cup superfine sugar
2 tbsp honey
1½ cups half and half
½ cup heavy cream
1 tsp almond extract
8oz (250g) mascarpone cheese

1 Put the tomatoes and raspberries in a glass bowl. Toss in the sugar and Amaretto. Chill until needed.

2 In a bowl, whisk together the egg yolks, sugar, and honey until smooth, pale, and thick.

3 To make the custard, gently heat the half and half, heavy cream, and almond extract to just below the boiling point. Add a little of the hot cream mixture to the egg yolk mixture, and whisk quickly to incorporate. Add a little more hot cream, and whisk again. Pour this mixture back into the saucepan, and stir constantly with a wooden spoon until the custard coats the back of the spoon. Remove from the heat. Whisk in the mascarpone until smooth, then cover and chill until cold.

4 Churn the custard in an ice cream maker for about 20 minutes or according to the manufacturer's instructions; then spoon into a freezerproof container. Carefully but thoroughly stir in the tomato and raspberry mixture, and freeze until firm. If you don't have an ice cream maker, combine the custard and mascarpone mixture in a container and freeze for 1 hour. Whisk well to break up any ice crystals, then repeat this process twice more. Incorporate the fruits, then freeze until firm. Remove from the freezer 15 minutes before needed, to allow it to soften a little.

Tommy Toe (p38)

Works well with
Cherry (pp36–51)
Standard globe (pp22–35)

Tomato and lemon marmalade

This simple marmalade can readily be made with red tomatoes, but use either yellow or brown ones if you have them. It will keep for up to 1 year if stored in a cool, dark place. Refrigerate after opening.

Makes about 3lb (1.5kg)
Prep time: 30 minutes
**Cooking time:
1½ hours**

5 large unwaxed lemons,
  zest peeled and cut into long,
  thin strips
2lb (1kg) tomatoes, peeled,
  cored, and cut into quarters
2lb (1kg) granulated sugar

1 Put the lemon strips in a small saucepan with a little water to cover. Simmer for 15 minutes, or until soft. Remove from the heat and set aside.

2 Cut the peeled lemons in half, and squeeze out all the juice, keeping any seeds. Set the juice aside. Scoop out any remaining flesh, and put in a glass or stainless steel bowl with the reserved seeds. Scoop out the seeds and juices from the tomato quarters, and put in the same bowl; mix well. Turn onto a piece of muslin, and tie tightly—this is your pectin bag.

3 Cut the tomato quarters into slices, mix with the lemon zest (and its cooking liquid), and turn into a large stainless steel saucepan. Measure the reserved lemon juice, and make up to 3¼ pints (1.8 liters) with cold water. Add this liquid to the pan, along with the pectin bag.

4 Bring the mixture to a boil, reduce the heat, and simmer for about 45 minutes, stirring occasionally, until it thickens and the zest is soft. Remove the bag, squeezing all the juice into the pan. Add the sugar, stir well and simmer gently for 20–30 minutes until setting point has been reached (left).

5 Ladle into hot, sterilized jars with tight-fitting lids, seal straight away, and label (pp142–143).

Testing for setting point
Remove from the heat and drop a teaspoon of the marmalade onto a clean, cold saucer. Let it cool, then push your finger into it—if the marmalade has formed a skin that "wrinkles," the setting point has been reached.

Brown Berry (p45)

Works well with
Cherry (pp36–51)
Standard globe (pp22–35)

Glossary

abscission layer – a zone of cells whose breakdown causes separation of a leaf or fruit from the stem

annual – a plant that completes its lifecycle in one growing season

bush – a plant that produces a number of sideshoots

calyx – the collective term for the green sepals of the flower that protect it in the bud stage and form a spiderlike structure on top of the ripe fruit

chlorophyll – the green plant pigment mainly responsible for light absorption

cell packs – individual containers used in multiples for sowing seeds

cordon – a plant generally restricted to one main stem

cotyledon – the first leaf or leaves to emerge after germination of a seed

cutworm – the larvae of various noctuid moths

cross-pollination – the transfer of pollen from the anther of a flower on one plant to the stigma of a flower on another plant

determinate plant – a bushy or dwarf tomato plant

dwarf – a plant that contains a dwarfing gene, making it very compact

F1 hybrid – the term stands for 'First filial generation' and refers to a cross of two pure breeding parental lines

fungus gnat – midgelike flies, up to $\frac{1}{8}$in (4mm)

genus – a category in plant classification between family and species

hybrid – a plant resulting from a cross between two distinct parents

heirloom – an old/treasured open-pollinated plant

indeterminate plant – tall or cordon plants that can grow to an indefinite length

knuckle – the point were the calyx of the tomato fruit joins the stem

leading shoot – the main, usually central, stem of a plant

leaf axil – the upper angle between a leaf and a stem

locule – a cavity or chamber within the fruit

loam – a term usually used imprecisely to denote a rich soil with a balanced mix of clay, sand, and humus

nematode – a worm-like animal also call an eelworm

open pollinated – seed produced from natural pollination, which can result in varied plants, although, as most tomatoes are self-fertile, their offspring tend to be consistent

perennial – any plant living for at least three growing seasons

photosynthesis – the process by which plants use sunlight to convert carbon dioxide and water into carbohydrates

pollen – male sex cells produced by stamens

pollination – the transfer of pollen from anthers to stigmas

potash – any of several compounds containing potassium

propagator – a structure providing a humid atmosphere for raising seedlings

semi-determinate plant – term usually used for cordons that grow to only 3–4ft (1–1.2m) or for those intermediate in growth habit between bush and cordon

sideshoot – a stem that arises from the side of a main shoot

Solanaceae – the plant family to which tomatoes and potatoes belong

species – a category in plant classification containing very similar individuals

stigma – the part of the female sex organ that receives pollen

truss – a compact cluster of flowers or fruits

variety – a grouping of plants having distinctive features that persist through successive generations

Useful resources

Burpee,
300 Park Avenue, Warminster, PA 18974
www.burpee.com

Johnny's Selected Seeds,
955 Benton Avenue, Winslow, MA 04901
www.johnnyseeds.com

Stokes Seeds Ltd.,
Box 548, Buffalo, NY 14240-0548
296 Collier Road, Box 10, Thorold,
ON L2V 5E9 Canada www.stokeseeds.com

Terra Edibles,
Village Green, 535 Ashley St., Foxboro, ON
K0B 2B0 Canada www.terraedibles.ca

Thompson & Morgan,
220 Faraday Avenue, Jackson, NJ 08527-5073 www.thompson-morgan.com

Tomato Growers Supply Co.,
P.O. Box 60015, Fort Meyer, FL 33906
www.tomatogrowers.com

Tomato Bob,
5764 Saucony Drive, Hilliard, OH 43026
www.tomatobob.com

Upper Canada Seeds,
44 Macklingate Court, Toronto, ON M1V 1A1
Canada www.uppercanadaseeds.ca

Veseys Seeds Ltd.,
P.O Box 9000, Charlottetown, PE C1A 8K6
www.veseys.com

Victory Seed Co.,
Box 192, Molalla, OR 97038
www.victoryseeds.com

Index

A

'Ailsa Craig' 32, 82
'Aker's West Virginia' 62
'Alaskan Fancy' 13, 66, 80
'Alicante' 24
'Amana Orange' 57
'The Amateur' 27
'Amish Paste' 81
'Amoroso' 50
'Ananas Noir' 13, 55
angora leaves 12
'Apero' 73
'Aunt Ruby's German
    Green' 53
'Aviro' 15, 66, 80
avocados: avocado,
    tomato, and lime salad
    180
    pico de gallo 154

B

bacterial leaf spot 117
baked beans 166
'Balconi Red' 44, 82
'Balconi Yellow' 44
basil and Parmesan
    stuffed tomatoes 162
beans, baked 166
beef: ragù bolognese 163
    slow-cooked beef cheeks
        with braised vegetables
        167
beef cheeks, slow-cooked
    with braised vegetables
    167
beefsteak tomatoes 13,
    52–63
bees 113
beets: tomato borscht 144
    Turkish shepherd's salad
    179

beta-carotene 15, 120
'Better Boy' 58
'Big Boy' 17, 58
'Big Rainbow' 63
'Big Zac' 126
bilocular fruits 13
'Black Cherry' 14, 38,
    80, 130
'Black Krim' 63
'Black Plum' 64
'Black Prince' 14
'Black Russian' 61
'Black Zebra' 26
blanching tomatoes 137
blight 81, 84, 114, 115,
    117, 119
'Blondköpfchen' 67
blossom end rot 115, 119
'Blue Ridge Mountain'
    20, 58
borage 104
borscht, tomato 144
'Brandywine' 14, 21, 59
bread: Mexican-style
    tomato summer pudding
    165
    tomato panade 168
breeding tomatoes
    130–31
'Broad Ripple Yellow
    Currant' 51
'Brown Berry' 45
bush tomatoes 10, 11
    in containers 82
    supports 84, 98

C

calcium 109
canning tomatoes 142,
    143 caponata 181
'Carmello' 14, 80

carotenoids 15
'Carters Fruit' 30
caterpillars 117
catfacing 119
'Cedrico' 126
'Celebrity' 29
char-grilling 140
charring, peeling tomatoes
    136
cheese: basil and
    Parmesan stuffed
        tomatoes 162
    melted feta on tomatoes
        and spinach 170
    tomato and Gruyère tart
        160
    tomato panade 168
'Cherokee Purple' 63
'Cherrola' 50
cherry tomatoes 13,
    36–51, 82
chiles: pico de gallo 154
    salsa de Molcajete
        154–5
'Chiquita' 73
chives 104, 105
'Chocolate Cherry' 39
chutneys 150
'Cleopatra' 126
climate 80–81
cloches 96
cocktail tomatoes 13
cold frames 96, 97
cold-tolerant plants 80
colors 13, 14, 120
comfrey fertilizer 109
companion planting
    104–5
compost 82, 88–9, 114
containers, growing
    tomatoes in 82–3,
    100–101

cooking techniques
    140–41
cordon tomatoes 10, 11
    in growing bags 82–3
    removing sideshoots
        110
    supports 84, 98
coring tomatoes 138
'Cornue des Andes' 16, 18,
    72
'Costoluto Fiorentino' 20,
    57, 81
'Costoluto Genovese' 56,
    81
'Country Taste' 52
cream of tomato soup 146
'Cristal' 34
crop rotation 102–3, 114
cross-pollination 10, 124,
    130
cucumber: gazpacho 152
'Cuor di Bue' 76
'Cuostralée' 54
curly top virus 117
currant tomatoes 13
cuttings 110–11
cutworms 99
'Czech's Excellent Yellow'
    33

D

'Dasher' 70
'De Colgar' 122
'Delicious' 57, 126
dicing tomatoes 135
disease-resistant plants
    114
diseases 81, 102, 104,
    114–19
'Dr. Wyche's Yellow' 52
dressings 177

'Druzba' 17, 32
drying seeds 125
drying tomatoes 142
dwarf tomatoes 10,
    11, 82

E

'Earl of Edgecombe' 32
'Early Cascade' 81
eggplants: caponata 181
'Elberta Girl' 12
'Elegance' 30
'Essex Wonder' 28
'Eva's Purple Ball' 17, 31
'Evergreen' 60
'Extra Sweetie' 10, 46

F

F1 hybrids 10, 90, 114,
    126
'Fantasio' 81
'Favorita' 15, 37
'Faworyt' 54
'Ferline' 23, 81, 114
fermenting seeds 125
fertilizers 109
'First In The Field' 30
'Flamme' 35
flavor 14
'Floridity' 14, 16, 19, 70
flowers, pollination 112
'Fox Cherry' 38
freezing tomatoes 143
frost 80, 86, 96, 122
fruits 13
    pests and diseases
        118–19
frying tomatoes 140
fungal diseases 81, 104,
    114, 117, 119

fungus gnats 104
fusarium wilts 114

G

'Garcia' 13
'Gardener's Delight' 42, 82
garlic: fresh tomatoes
    marinaded with 176
    roasted tomato and
        garlic soup 156
'Gartenperle' 37
gazpacho 152
'German Pink' 21, 61
germination 92, 124
ghost spots 119
'Glacier' 23, 80
globe tomatoes 22–35
gnats, fungus 104
'Gold Medal' 62
'Gold Rush' 51
'Golden Cherry' 15, 39
'Golden Gem' 21, 36
'Golden Pearl' 47
'Golden Sunrise' 31
'Golden Sweet' 69
grafting 128–9
'Great White' 81
'Green Bell Pepper' 77
'Green Sausage' 12, 77
'Green Tiger' 47
'Green Zebra' 14, 26
greenback 119
greenhouses 86
grilling tomatoes 140
'Grosse Lisse' 29
growing bags 82–3,
    100–101
growth habits 10–11

H

'Halladay's Mortgage
    Lifter' 54
hanging baskets 82–3,
    100
hardening off 96–7
hardiness 80–81
harvesting 120–23
'Harzfeuer' 35
hawkmoth 117
health benefits 15
heat-tolerant plants 81
heirloom varieties 10, 90
'Hillbilly Potato Leaf' 12,
    53
'Homestead' 81
hybrid varieties 10
hygiene 114

I

ice cream, tomato and
    mascarpone 182
'Ildi' 12, 73
insects, pollination
    112–13

J

'Jack Hawkins' 56
'Japanese Black Trifele' 75
'Jasper' 44
'Jelly Bean' 40
'Jersey Giant' 67
'Jubilee' 10, 22
'Juliet' 16, 69

K

'Kellogg's Breakfast' 60
ketchup 158
knives 134

L

leaf roll virus 117
leaves 12
    pests and diseases
        116–17
'Legend' 55, 81, 114
lemon: tomato and lemon
    marmalade 185
'Lemon Boy' 35, 114
light, greenhouses 86
locules 13
'Long Keeper' 33
long-keeper varieties 122
'Long Tom' 16, 19, 67
'Loveheart' 19, 21, 41
lycopene 15, 120

M

magnesium deficiency
    117
'Marglobe' 81
marigolds 104, 105
marinara-style sauce 153
marmalade, tomato and
    lemon 185
marrow, pan-fried with
    green tomatoes 172
'Maskotka' 17, 46
'Matt's Wild Cherry' 39
Mexican-style tomato
    summer pudding 165
'Micro-Tom' 43, 82
microclimates 80
minerals 15, 109
'Mini-Charm' 70
mini-plum tomatoes 13
'Minibel' 82
mint 104, 105
'Moneymaker' 24
moths 104, 117
mulching 106–7

'Mule Team' 17, 25, 81
multilocular fruits 13
mycorrhizae 104

N

nasturtiums 104, 105
'Nectar' 13, 19, 42
nematodes 102, 104, 114
nettle fertilizer 109
nitrogen 109

O

'Old Ivory Egg' 70
'Olivade' 64
'Omar's Lebanese' 126
'Orange Banana' 72
'Orange Pixie' 26
'Orange Strawberry' 76
organic matter 88–9, 101
organic mulches 106, 107

P

pan-frying tomatoes 140
'Pantano' 56
pasta with fresh tomato
    sauce 149
patio pots 82
peach, tomato, and
    strawberry salad 174
peat 82
peeling tomatoes 136–7
pelleted seeds 90
'Pepe' 45
peppers: gazpacho 152
    tomato chutney with
        pimentón and 150
pests 102, 114–19
phosphorus 109
'Piccolo' 50

pico de gallo 154
'Picolino' 47
'Pineapple (Ananas)' 53
'Pink Accordion' 55, 80, 81
'Pink Ping Pong' 29
pizza, simple marinara-
    style sauce for 153
planting tomatoes
    98–101
plantlets 91, 114
'Plum Lemon' 75
plum tomatoes 13, 64–73
'Polar Baby' 80
pollination 112–13, 124,
    130
polytunnels 86–7
potagers 84
potassium 109, 126
potato-leafed plants 12
prawns: Mexican-style
    tomato summer pudding
    165
preparing tomatoes 134–9
preserving tomatoes
    142–3
pricking out seedlings 94,
    95
'Principe Borghese' 18, 66
pruning sideshoots 110
'Purple Calabash' 60
'Purple Russian' 68

R

ragù bolognese 163
raised beds 101
raspberries, tomato and
    mascarpone ice cream
    with 182
red cabbage: Turkish
    shepherd's salad 179
'Red Cherry' 40

'Red Fig' 75
'Red Pigmy' 48
'Reisetomate' 21, 77
'Riesentraube' 21, 49
ring culture 82
'Rio Grande' 65
ripening tomatoes 14,
    120, 122–3
roasting tomatoes 140
'Roma' 10, 65, 81, 114
'Roncardo' 22
root-knot nematodes 102,
    114
rootstocks, grafting 128
'Rosada' 19, 70
'Rose de Berne' 61
'Ruby' 18, 48
'Rudolph' 18, 70

S

'Sakura' 42
salads 20–21
    avocado, tomato,
        and lime salad 180
    melted feta on tomatoes
        and spinach 170
    tomato, peach, and
        strawberry salad 174
    tomato salad with
        tarragon, lemon zest,
        and capers 173
    Turkish shepherd's salad
        179
salsas 17
    pico de gallo 154
    salsa de Molcajete
        154–5
    salsa romesco 147
'San Marzano Lungo' 16,
    18, 65
'Santa' 13

sauces 16
    fresh tomato sauce 149
    ketchup 158
    simple marinara-style
        sauce for pizza 153
    sofrito 157
Savi's fresh tomato
    chutney 150–51
'Scotland Yellow' 28, 80
seed chambers 13
seeding tomatoes 139
seedlings 94–5
seeds 90
    breeding tomatoes 130
    saving 124–5
    seeding tomatoes 139
    sowing 92–3
semi-bush tomatoes 10
shading greenhouses 86
shelter 101
'Shirley' 23
shows 126
'Siberian' 10, 34, 80
sideshoots, removing
    110–11, 114
'Silvery Fir Tree' 12, 28
'Sioux' 25
skin: peeling tomatoes
    136–7
    splitting 108, 119
'Slankards' 126
slicing tomatoes 135
smoking tomatoes 143
'Snowberry' 14, 40
sofrito 157
soil: crop rotation 102
    disease prevention 114
    enriching 88–9
    fallow seasons 102
    mulching 106–7
    planting tomatoes 98–9
soups 18–19

cream of tomato soup 146

gazpacho 152

roasted tomato and garlic soup 156

tomato borscht 144

sowing seeds 92–3

'Speckled Roman' 68

spinach, melted feta on tomatoes and 170

splitting 108, 119

sterilizing bottles 142

'Sterling Old Norway' 14

'Stone' 81

storing seeds 124

strawberries: tomato, peach, and strawberry salad 174

'Striadel' 43

'Stupice' 17, 27, 80

'Sub-Arctic Plenty' 34, 80, 96

sugar content 14

'Suncherry Premium' 45

'Sungella' 24

'Sungold' 41

sunscald 119

'Sunset' 41

'Sunstream' 72

'Supermarmande' 20, 59

supports 84, 98, 100–101

'Sweet Pea' 51

T

'Tamina' 27

tart, tomato and Gruyère 160

temperatures: hardiness 80–81

pollination 112

ripening 120

'Thessaloniki' 81

thinning seedlings 94

'Tigerella' 25

'Tiny Tim' 10, 37

tomato and Gruyère tart 160

tomato and lemon marmalade 185

tomato and mascarpone ice cream 182

tomato borscht 144

tomato hornworm 117

tomato mosaic virus 117

tomato panade 168

tomato, peach, and strawberry salad 174

tomato salad with tarragon, lemon zest, and capers 173

'Tomatoberry' 19, 46

'Tommy Toe' 38

'Totem' 33

transpiration 108

trilocular fruits 13

'Tropic' 81

'Tumbler' 10, 36, 82, 130

'Tumbling Tom Red' 49, 82

'Tumbling Tom Yellow' 49

tunnel cloches 96

Turkish shepherd's salad 179

V

'Vandos' 126

'Variegated' 12

'Velvet Red' 12, 43

ventilation, greenhouses 86

verticillium wilts 114

vitamins 15

W

wall o'water 96

walls, growing tomatoes against 101

watering 99, 108

weather 80–81

weeds 106, 114

wet-tolerant plants 81

'White Tomesol' 31

whitefly 86, 104, 115, 117

wild tomatoes 6

wilts 114

windbreaks 101

Y

'Yellow Ailsa Craig' 28

'Yellow Butterfly' 68

'Yellow Oxheart' 76

'Yellow Pear' 74

'Yellow Pigmy' 20, 48

'Yellow Santa' 69

'Yellow Stuffer' 74

Acknowledgments

Dorling Kindersley would like to thank: Siobhan O'Connor for her excellent recipe editing; Annelise Evans for all her editorial help; Carolyn Hewitson and Kenny Grant for their design assistance; Graham Rae, William Reavell, Howard Rice, and Sarah Ashun for the excellent photography; Jo Walton, Romaine Werblow, and Karen Forsythe for their picture research; Katie Giovanni, the food stylist, for her expertise; Sue Rowlands, the prop stylist; Jim Buckland, Sarah Wain, and Shirley Tasker at West Dean Gardens, Sussex, for allowing us to photograph their wonderful tomato collection; Jane, Amanda, and Lesley at Not Just Food for their efficient testing; Hilary Bird for creating the index; and the following for their kind donation of tomatoes: Jane and Matt Simpson at Simpson's Seeds, Kieran Devine at Wight Salads Group; Jim Arbury at Wisley Gardens; Sharon MacGregor at De Ruiter Seeds; Mike Thurlow at Audley End; Terry Marshall; Pennard Plants; Bernard Sparkes at Melrow Salads; and Jessica Tsang.

Gail Harland would like to thank: Andrew Roff at Dorling Kindersley for editing with great good humor and photographers Graham Rae and the multi-talented Howard Rice. Many people at seed firms, particularly Caroline Rush at Thompson and Morgan. Grateful thanks also go to my sons Ashley and Jonathan who have been chief tasters of a range of sometimes strange tomatoes over the years. Somehow they still seem to believe that tomatoes should be round and red.

Sofia Larrinua-Craxton would like to thank: Savi Sperl for her endless enthusiasm; Barbara and Gaetano Mansi, for sharing the Ragu recipe; Cecilia Gutierrez Elizondo, for making that memorable gazpacho, which we loved so much; Antonella Tagliapietra and Philip Oakes for their hospitality at Arte Culinaria and for the recipe for beef cheeks; New Covent Garden Food Co. for giving me the chance to do so much work in the UK and USA, thanks also go to you for the Tomato Borscht recipe; Eric, Rosie, Sally, and everyone at Books for Cooks—you are wonderful!; MC, Andrew, and everyone at DK; to all my family, including Merida who wanted her name printed "in my next book"; and last but not least I'd like to thank my husband Oliver to whom I would like to dedicate my share of this book.